CW00505989

PEP
GUARDIOLA

NOTES ON A SEASON

PEP
GUARDIOLA

NOTES ON A SEASON

Reach Sport

www.reachsport.com

First published in Great Britain in 2022 by
Reach Sport, 5 St Paul's Square, Liverpool, L3 9SJ.

www.reachsport.com
@reach_sport

Reach Sport is a part of Reach plc.
One Canada Square, Canary Wharf, London, E15 5AP.

ISBN: 9781914197635

Compiled by: Nick Moreton
Introduction by: Rob Pollard
Artwork by: Rick Cooke

Printed and bound by CPI Group (UK) Ltd,
Croydon, CR0 4YY.

NOTES ON A SEASON

2021-22

PREMIER LEAGUE DOMINANCE CONTINUES WITH ANOTHER REMARKABLE CAMPAIGN UNDER GUARDIOLA'S GUIDANCE

THE Premier League is widely considered to be the most competitive domestic league in world football.

For ten years between 2009-2019, the title changed hands every season. In fact, at that stage it had only been retained on seven occasions in 26 years.

But Manchester City have now won four in five seasons, a statistic that underlines the remarkable consistency the team has shown under Pep Guardiola's management.

The Catalan has changed everything. Not only are

City now habitual winners, collecting a remarkable 11 major trophies since his arrival in 2016, but the entire makeup of the club has been revolutionised, too. He has introduced a beautiful style of football now embedded across all age groups of the City Football Academy, and a winning mentality exists where previously there had been fragility. In so many ways, the club is unrecognisable to the one he inherited.

City's latest Premier League success was sealed in dramatic, heart-stopping circumstances.

Another titanic battle with Jurgen Klopp's Liverpool saw Guardiola's side enter the final day of the 2021-22 Premier League campaign knowing a win over Aston Villa would seal the title. However, despite heading into the game in fine form, City delivered an uncharacteristically below-par performance and were 2-0 down with 14 minutes remaining.

It looked as though a gruelling ten months would end in devastation for a side few could argue had consistently produced the finest football in the land.

It happened so suddenly, but what followed – three goals in five barely believable minutes – turned everything on its head and City, somehow, were champions again. Cue pandemonium and delirium in the stands at the Etihad, with the outpouring of emotion from Guardiola at full-time telling its own story of a draining campaign.

In terms of drama, City's 2012 title victory – known

as 93:20 to denote the time of Sergio Aguero's last-gasp goal – will probably never be beaten, but this was about as close as you can get.

"Today was so special," Guardiola said afterwards. "Four Premier League titles – these guys are legends already; people have to admit it. This group of players are absolutely eternal in this club because what we achieved is so difficult."

Guardiola is right. That kind of consistency, in the face of a fierce rivalry with Liverpool, is remarkable and deserving of widespread praise. This City team is going down in history.

Indeed, Liverpool's role in City's recent flurry of titles shouldn't be underestimated. Their excellence has forced Guardiola and his backroom staff to constantly find improvements. The two sides have pushed one another and changed the landscape of English football. One look at a list of highest points tallies in Premier League history tells you everything, with Guardiola's City and Klopp's Liverpool occupying the top four places with two apiece.

"I want to congratulate Liverpool for what they've done," Guardiola said after sealing this year's title. "The magnitude of our achievement is because of the magnitude of this rival. That makes us feel more proud because we know which team we face and we are incredibly happy."

The day after the win over Villa, Guardiola and his squad paraded across Manchester city centre in three open top busses. After two years badly affected by the COVID-19 health pandemic, seeing the Premier League trophy held aloft with fans lining the streets felt like more than simply a celebration of a successful football team.

Elsewhere, it was another solid campaign for City. Guardiola's men reached the semi-final of the UEFA Champions League only to lose in heart-breaking fashion to Real Madrid, whilst their FA Cup aspirations ended at the same stage with defeat to Liverpool.

This book is a reminder of every step taken in each competition through Guardiola's pre-match programme notes and post-match interviews – another memorable season for City told through the words of their great manager and one of the game's most innovative thinkers.

This is Pep Guardiola's *Notes On A Season*.

AUG

2021

With six points picked up from the nine on offer in August, a disappointing opening day of the Premier League season was quickly forgotten as fans returned to the Etihad to see the goals start flowing once again

15th: Tottenham Hotspur (PL) A
21st: Norwich City (PL) H
28th: Arsenal (PL) H

Sunday, August 15
Premier League
Tottenham Hotspur 1, Manchester City 0

Line-up: Ederson, Cancelo, Dias, Ake, Mendy (Zinchenko 78),
Fernandinho (c), Gundogan, Grealish, Sterling (Jesus 70),
Torres, Mahrez (De Bruyne 78).
Subs not used: Steffen, Walker, Stones, Laporte, Rodrigo, Bernardo.

City's 2021/22 Premier League campaign got off to a disappointing start as we suffered an opening day defeat at Tottenham Hotspur.

Son Heung-Min's 55th minute strike ultimately proved the difference and was enough to hand the hosts all three points as our Tottenham Hotspur Stadium hoodoo continued.

City had our chances – especially in a dominant first 15 minutes – but we failed to make that early pressure tell and ultimately it proved to be an afternoon of frustration for Pep Guardiola's reigning champions.

Pep's post-match reaction: 'We started really well and after 20 minutes we allowed them too much running in transition. With Son, Bergwijn and Lucas Moura, we wanted to avoid it. In general, we showed a good spirit and good intention and we arrived in the final third many times, but we could not be clinical enough. Son scores and we lose. We need to be more precise. Teams are waiting to punish us. But I see in the game many, many good things. I know the result wasn't what we wanted but I saw things that will make us better.'

Post-match notes

With all the focus and attention on Jack Grealish on what was his City Premier League debut, despite the result there were plenty of encouraging signs of what to expect from the England attacking midfielder. Always full of intent and confidence, the 25-year-old looked to attack at every opportunity and never backed down even in the face of some full-blooded challenges. There were also several instances of some exciting link-up play with the likes of Raheem Sterling and Ilkay Gundogan which only augurs well.

**v Norwich
Saturday, August 21**

'I AM SO EXCITED ABOUT THE SEASON AND ABOUT WHAT WE CAN ACHIEVE'

Premier League

TODAY is our first home game of the season – and, most importantly, the first game at the Etihad with a full stadium since February 2020.

Honestly, it will be a pleasure to have you all with us once again, we have missed you so much. Football is not the same without you guys to share it with us.

Today's match will be a special moment for us all. The players will feel your support, their adrenaline will be higher, and the game will be better as a result of you being here, I have no doubt about that.

This afternoon we welcome Norwich City to the Etihad, a side I admire a lot.

They were the best team in the Championship last season and totally deserve to be back in the Premier League. To get 97 points in such a difficult division says everything about the quality and mentality of Daniel Farke's side.

It should be a fantastic game and I am really looking forward to it.

It's not been an easy pre-season for us with many of our guys not arriving back until recently following Euro 2020 and the Copa America, but the players are definitely getting fitter and sharper every day. I have seen so many good things in the training sessions, and my players arrived back in top condition.

The result in our opening Premier League game away at Tottenham Hotspur last weekend was a difficult one for us all but the way we started showed me that the team is there. We played with personality, and we arrived many times, we just could not score.

Of course, we know the quality of the Premier League and we know that every match is so, so tough.

But there were many, many good things about the way we played. I know the result wasn't what we wanted but I saw things that will make us better.

Now all the guys are back here together, and we need to continue to keep working hard day by day, training well, looking to improve and preparing for every challenge.

We know that against Norwich that we need to produce a good game and we will try everything to get the three points.

Looking ahead generally, I am very excited about the season and about what we can achieve.

I am a very lucky guy because I have a fantastic group of players. But ever since I arrived in England, I always get the feeling the quality gets better and better every single year. And I have no doubt that will be the case again, so that means we need to try to be better than we were last season.

We are the champions right now and we have the Premier League trophy in our cabinet.

But now we have to go again and fight our very hardest to reclaim our crown. Our rivals want to beat us, and we have to be ready to meet that challenge.

The important thing is that the players have 90 minutes in the legs after the Tottenham game and we have had another vital week working together to prepare to play Norwich.

I am sure the players can come back step by step and that with your backing and support we will only get stronger and stronger.

Enjoy the game and thank you so much for your continued support. It means a lot to myself, the players and everyone at the Club.

Manchester City 5, Norwich 0

Goals: Krul (7 og), Grealish (22), Laporte (64), Sterling (71), Mahrez (84)

Line-up: Ederson, Walker, Dias, Laporte, Cancelo, Silva, Rodrigo, Gundogan (Palmer 69), Jesus, Torres (Sterling 61), Grealish (Mahrez 75).
Subs not used: Ake, Zinchenko, Steffen, Mendy, Fernandinho, Doyle.

City bounced back from last weekend's defeat at Spurs to comprehensively beat Norwich 5-0 at the Etihad.

There was a feeling of business as usual as the champions went about dismantling the Canaries, with a couple of goals before the break and three more in the second half.

After an own goal opened the scoring, Jack Grealish

marked his home debut with his first goal for the Club.

Aymeric Laporte added a third before second half subs Raheem Sterling and Riyad Mahrez ensured it was a five-star performance for our first home game in front of a full house for almost 18 months.

Pep's post-match reaction: 'This result was the consequence of how many good things we have done. We are still not at the top – there are still many things to do. We trained, we were refreshed, happy for these first points... hopefully they will not be the last! One of the reasons why I'm a manager is when you can work with people and humans like Gabriel. He never complains, he plays five minutes, he plays the best five minutes he can do. He's happy on left, right or centre and today the connection with Kyle was exceptional. I'm pleased with his performance; he was involved in three of our goals and is an incredibly important player for us. He made an exceptional performance today, and I repeat, if he plays three minutes he plays the best three minutes for the club and everyone. The more you have in this position the better we are. When someone plays like this they deserve to play He's so young, big congratulations because he deserves in life the best. He's so generous and as I say, I'm incredibly satisfied for him.'

v Arsenal
Saturday, August 28

'FANS GIVE US SUCH A BOOST – THEY ARE EVERYTHING TO US'

Premier League

WELCOME back to the Etihad Stadium. It was only a week ago we were here with a full crowd for the first time in 18 months when we played Norwich. What a difference you guys made for that game. Honestly, I want you all to know that the players, myself and my staff loved having you back with us. You make everything so much more exciting, and you really lifted the occasion. So thank you to all of you and hopefully you will do the same for us again today.

I was very pleased with our performance against Norwich. I saw so many good things. The players looked happy, refreshed and we showed real quality in every position. We were all delighted to get three points and hopefully now we can build on that performance.

We have trained well again this week. It's been great to get everyone together at CFA and work on our fitness and tactics as a group. I can sense my players are getting sharper, and they are hungry for success, which is good. I am so lucky to manage this squad because always they are so professional and dedicated to their work. They are a credit to Manchester City.

And now we welcome Arsenal and my friend Mikel Arteta to the Etihad. Always as a manager you look forward to big games and this is definitely a big game. With all their history and the quality of their players, it is always a great occasion when we face them.

Mikel is someone I know well from our time working

together at City. He did so much good work for us and helped us achieve our targets while he was here. I will always be grateful to him, and I know the way he sets his team up means we will be in for a tough game today.

I am so excited about this season and what we can achieve. The players know exactly what we expect of them and how we want to play. This group has been through so much together and learned so much over the past few seasons, I can't wait to see what they can produce this season. Those experiences we have had and the history we have created will help us – but we know this is a new season and we must go again, work hard every single day and be the best we can be.

And today we unveil statues for Vincent Kompany and David Silva. These two players have done so much for this football club. They helped create the cycle of success we are in now and without them, all we have done in the last few years would not have been possible. It is absolutely right that they will be honoured in this way.

Enjoy the game, everyone. It should be a fantastic 90 minutes.

Manchester City 5, Arsenal 0

Goals: Gundogan (7), Torres (12, 84), Jesus (43), Rodrigo (53)

Line-up: Ederson, Walker (Zinchenko 46), Cancelo, Dias, Laporte, Rodrigo, Gundogan, Bernardo (Sterling 58), Grealish, Torres, Jesus (Mahrez 62). Subs not used: Steffen, Stones, Ake, Fernandinho, Doyle, Palmer.

City made it back-to-back 5-0 home wins this season with another stellar display at the Etihad.

The champions were three up by the break, with Gunners reduced to ten men with a dangerous challenge from Granit Xhaka earning a straight red card.

Ilkay Gundogan, Ferran Torres (2), Gabriel Jesus and Rodri were all on target.

Pep's post-match reaction: 'We have a fantastic squad. Thank you to the scouting department from day one for the players they have given me. We found a goal without deserving it and after we went 2-0 up and they had a player sent off, the game was different. It was lovely day and amazing atmosphere, easier for us, tough for the opposition. We would have preferred to have nine points, but what is important is not what we have done. OK, we have six points right now from just three fixtures, but we feel these last two weeks have helped us a lot to work again with our basics and our principles. And the people day by day and the way that they train in these two or three days, I'm really impressed. I said to the players: 'Continue like this guys.' I'm not glad with the result, it's the way they behave every single day. Now it is non-stop. They go away with the international squads and come back hopefully fit with no injuries. And you see the schedule for September. We have to be ready. Because what is coming is a tough, tough, tough period for us.'

SEP

2021

The month in which Pep Guardiola became our most successful manager ever. Unbeaten in the Premier League, September also saw us reach a significant Champions League milestone and our Carabao Cup defence get off to a flyer

11th: Leicester City (PL) A
15th: RB Leipzig (CL) H
18th: Southampton (PL) H
21st: Wycombe Wanderers (CC) H
25th: Chelsea (PL) A
28th: Paris Saint Germain (CL) A

Saturday, September 11
Premier League
Leicester City 0, Manchester City 1

Goals: Silva (62)

Line-up: Ederson, Walker, Dias, Laporte, Cancelo, Rodrigo, Gundogan, Bernardo, Jesus (Fernandinho 84), Grealish, Torres (Sterling 64). Subs not used: Carson, Stones, Ake, Zinchenko, De Bruyne, Mahrez, Foden.

Bernardo Silva scored the only goal of the game to give Manchester City a deserved, but hard-earned victory against Leicester City at the King Power Stadium.

The Portuguese midfielder lashed home from close range in the 62nd minute after Joao Cancelo's strike deflected kindly into his path off Caglar Soyuncu to give Pep Guardiola's men a third consecutive victory.

It was just reward for City, who dominated an entertaining contest in which the home side saw a couple of golden opportunities go begging before Bernardo broke the deadlock.

Pep's post-match reaction: 'It was an excellent performance. After an international break you always have doubts, but the mentality from the players was incredible from the first minute to the end. After the international break it is not one of the best places to come. We played really well. We conceded few [chances], we created a lot and unfortunately we could not score more goals, but the big signal to be solid during one season is the way we played. Some moments were difficult, we knew it. Always we suffer against Leicester. It was the same in the Community Shield, we had a good game. Today was different, we were able to win. The last three games we were incredibly good and that's why our victories are there.'

Post-match notes

This was a third impressive performance on the trot for Bernardo Silva, who was one of our key men in the opening weeks of the season. Here, he was our brightest attacking threat, causing the Foxes countless problems with both his passing and driving runs.

On Champions League preparations...

The last three weeks was so good. The way we trained was a little bit of a surprise after what we achieved last season. They know exactly what we want to do, what we want to practice, and I think the mechanism is much better.

That's why, the way we trained after Tottenham, we started long weeks together for the first time, I saw many, many good things that the results are here.

Hopefully we can continue with this mentality and raise the standards through the training sessions. That's the key point. That's what we have to work on in the next weeks.

Pep Guardiola

'I WANT THE PLAYERS TO LEARN FROM LAST SEASON AND TRY TO GO ONE STEP FURTHER'

UEFA Champions League

GOOD evening everyone and welcome to the Etihad Stadium for our first Champions League match of the season. It should be a fantastic occasion.

I want to extend a warm welcome to all the RB Leipzig players and staff here this evening. We hope you enjoy playing here for the first time.

Leipzig are a top team with top players, and we know how hard this game will be.

I know really well the rhythm, the quality and the pace they have.

The Bundesliga is a league I know so well. It's incredibly strong and Leipzig have been competing at the top for the last five years. They are consistent, with quality all over the pitch. It will be a good test, and it is so important we go into the game with the right attitude.

I really cannot wait for kick off because always you want to test yourself against the best.

And that's what we will have to do in all the games we play in this group. I say every single year that qualifying from the group stage of the Champions League is a huge achievement, given the quality of the opposition. That will be the case more than ever if we can manage it this season because in this group we have to face three of the best teams in the competition. It will be incredibly difficult.

My players continue to make me proud. It was so

important to win at Leicester and I was delighted with the way we played. It was an excellent performance. Always the first game back after an international break is difficult – but the mentality of my players was clear. They were incredible all the way through that game. I am so lucky to be their manager because their attitude is always so good.

We only conceded a few chances and we created so many. Okay, we would like to have scored more goals – always we want more – but we looked so solid and stable, which is great to see at this stage of a season.

We score goals as a team, that is one of our strengths, so to see nine different players score in our last three games is fantastic for us and, if we continue in that way, we will win games this season, that's for sure.

We made so much progress in this competition last season. I know the result in the final was not what we wanted, but the players showed so much courage and intelligence to get to Porto and I was so proud of the way we played throughout.

I want the players to learn from what we did and take it into this season and try to go one step further. Always we are trying to improve, trying to find those extra details that can make us better.

Again, I want to say the support we have had in the first two home games of the season has been fantastic – and those who were at Leicester on Saturday, you were amazing! To have fans back is making everything so much more exciting. Thank you for your support.

Enjoy the game.

Manchester City 6, RB Leipzig 3

Goals: Ake (16), Mukiele (28 og), Mahrez (47), Grealish (56), Cancelo (75), Jesus (85)

Line-up: Ederson, Cancelo, Dias, Ake, Zinchenko, Rodrigo (Fernandinho 59), De Bruyne (Foden 71) Bernardo (Gundogan 59), Mahrez, Grealish (Jesus 81), Torres (Sterling 71).
Subs not used: Carson, Slicker, Walker, Sterling, Palmer, Lavia.

Nathan Ake and Jack Grealish scored for the first time in the Champions League as Manchester City got the better of RB Leipzig in a nine-goal thriller to ensure we made a positive start to our group stage campaign.

With supporters back at the Etihad Stadium for a European tie for the first time since November 2019, Pep Guardiola's men recorded a remarkable 6-3 victory to become the quickest English team to reach 50 wins in the competition.

Ake broke the deadlock with a towering header from a Grealish corner before Nordi Mukiele headed into his own net to extend our advantage.

Christopher Nkunku brought the visitors back into the game with a six yard header, but our two goal lead was restored before half-time when Riyad Mahrez netted from the penalty spot.

Following the break, Nkunku reduced the deficit once more but Guardiola's men hit back immediately as Grealish capped a fine performance with a stunning goal on his Champions League debut.

Nkunku's third threatened a tense finale, but Joao Cancelo's 25-yard thunderbolt gave us breathing space again, before Gabriel Jesus tapped in at the far post on his 200th club appearance to after former City man Angelino was sent off for a second bookable offence.

Pep's post-match reaction: 'I am delighted and happy and thank you to these incredible players we have. It was a really tough game. They are able to create chances, they attack you in the build-up and they defend the spaces inside really well. The first game at home it was important to win and we scored six goals. Seventeen goals in the last four games is nice to give to them. Now we rest and prepare for Southampton. Nine goals in one game so it is nice for all the people watching. A team like RB Leipzig never gives up. They have a clear idea. They attack inside, they put a lot of players inside. They don't have the problem of losing the ball because when they lose the ball they make quick transitions. When we have the ball they are there to press you. At the same time when you can regain the ball, pass back and switch play a little bit, you always have a chance to run and score a goal. I think the game was tight. We were fortunate that when they scored we were able to score immediately. I saw the game against Bayern Munich, they made it 1-2 and Bayern Munich suffered because of the counter-

*attack. It is an interesting team. They have played like this
since Ralph Rangnick arrived. They really play. It is one of the
best teams in Germany. That is why I am incredibly satisfied
with the players for the first victory in the group stage. We have
an outstanding squad. From day one until now they give me
exceptional players with a very good mentality. We are the same
guys as last season, just changed Sergio for Jack. Last season we
were able to score goals. We don't have a player who can score
25 goals. The last week we had many players in the box and
that helped to score goals."*

Post-match notes

Jack Grealish became the first Englishman to both
score and assist on his Champions League debut since
Wayne Rooney versus Fenerbahce in September 2004.
With Paris Saint-Germain and Club Brugge playing out a
1-1 draw in the other game in Group A, this victory meant
City sat top after the opening round of fixtures. Our
victory over RB Leipzig also saw us become the fastest
English team in history to reach 50 Champions League
wins. The victory over Jesse Marsch's side was our 50th
in 91 games. Only Real Madrid reached a half century
quicker, with their 50 in 88 matches, achieved in 2003,
the current record. Our 50 wins in 91 matches is quicker
than Barcelona, Paris Saint-Germain and Manchester
United.

**v Southampton
Saturday, September 18**

'IT HAS BEEN A PRIVILEGE AND A PLEASURE TO BE YOUR MANAGER FOR EVERY SINGLE ONE OF MY 300 MATCHES'

HELLO again! It's a very quick turnaround between home games this week, with our win over RB Leipzig just three days ago.

It was a very tough game against Leipzig. Always when you face teams from the top of the Bundesliga, it is a huge challenge. I was delighted with the way we played. These incredible players I have make this job so rewarding and they continue to impress me with their quality and dedication.

It is always so important to win home matches and to score lots of goals against a top team is obviously very special. We have scored a lot of goals recently, which is really positive for us. It shows we are doing a lot of good things.

RB Leipzig never, not for one second, gave up. They have such a clear way of playing and attack with lots of players. We know the return game against them in Germany will be incredibly difficult and we will be better prepared now having played against them.

I say this every season but getting through the group stage is my only focus in the Champions League right now. Last season we improved so much in this competition, but we have started again now and we must play one game at a time and make sure we get into the draw for the last-16. That is all that matters. To start with a win is brilliant, but there is still a lot of work to do.

My players deserved a day to rest and recover after the Leipzig match, but then our focus immediately switched to Southampton, which is another very important game for us.

I want to extend a really warm welcome to Ralph Hasenhüttl, his staff and his players. Today should be a great occasion because Southampton always look to play good football. It is a pleasure to play against them.

Like Leipzig, Southampton have a really clear idea of how they want to play. They have a lot of pace and I am sure they will try to attack. It should be another entertaining game.

I have discussed this with my players in the days after the Leipzig win and we will be ready. There is no doubt this match will also be difficult, and we must be prepared to fight for everything.

As some of you will know, the game against Leipzig was my 300th game in charge at City. It is really special for me to have been here for so many games. I just wanted to say it's been a huge privilege and a pleasure to be the Manchester City manager for every single one of those matches.

Thank you so much for your continued support. It means so much to me, the players and everyone working here at City.

Enjoy today's game!

Manchester City 0, Southampton 0

Line-up: Ederson, Walker, Dias, Ake, Cancelo, Fernandinho (De Bruyne 65), Gundogan, Bernardo (Foden 72), Sterling, Grealish, Jesus (Mahrez 67).
Subs not used: Carson, Torres, Mbete, Palmer, Lavia, Wilson-Esbrand.

Manchester City's remarkable goalscoring run came to an end after the defending Premier League champions were held to a goalless draw against Southampton.

Pep Guardiola's side came into the game having scored 17 goals in our previous four outings, but were frustrated by the Saints' spirited performance at the Etihad Stadium.

In stark contrast to the midweek win over RB Leipzig, this was a relatively low-key affair, which hinged on two VAR decisions.

Raheem Sterling thought he had scored a 90th minute winner when he reacted quickest to turn in the rebound after substitute Phil Foden's header was saved, but City's joy proved short lived as the video check agreed the assistant referee had correctly flagged for offside.

Pep's post-match reaction: 'Today we didn't win not because we don't have a centre-forward. We didn't win because the process to build up, to create, to give better balls to the players up front was not good. When it is good, you can run, you arrive in better positions. Of course, we had just one shot on target, but there were four or five blocked in the six-yard box, so we were there

That is not the reason [we didn't win]. The reason is because we didn't do the process for our back four and Fernandinho. The five guys who have to bring the ball to the other players was not good today. There are many ways to score a goal. You can be set back and counter-attack or you can be direct. Our process is the goalkeeper passes to the central defenders, the central defenders pass to the full-backs, they pass to the holding midfielders, the attacking midfielders pass the ball to the wingers. In that process, we travel, we fly, we live all together to make the transition. This is our way. This process from the beginning was not perfectly what we wanted. It was difficult sometimes because the opponent was good. They defended well. Sometimes it is difficult and the opponent is involved in that. We cannot forget that. Sometimes we need more time to train, to practice. Today was like this. We struggled for the first 15 minutes in each half, but in the last 30 minutes we were better.'

Post-match notes

Raheem Sterling made his 200th Premier League appearance for City, the ninth player to reach that tally for the Club, and only the second Englishman after Joe Hart.

v Wycombe Wanderers
Tuesday, September 21

'WE TAKE EVERY GAME SERIOUSLY, NO MATTER WHO THE OPPOSITION ARE OR WHAT THE COMPETITION IS'

Carabao Cup

Good evening, everyone. Tonight we begin our Carabao Cup campaign and I am very excited to get started. We have enjoyed so many great days in this competition over the past four years and it has provided us with a platform to go on and win other trophies. It's been very important to us.

Since I came to City, we have taken every game seriously, no matter what the competition or who the opposition are. If not, it would be impossible to win four Carabao Cups in a row. I am proud of our record in all the English trophies. We have been so consistent and that's all down to the dedication and profession-alism of my players. Our approach to this will never change.

It's also a competition that has allowed us to use some of our Academy players and I want that to continue. We have some fantastic young players at Manchester City and giving them a chance to play senior football is very important for their development.

It's a chance for them to feel the physicality and pace of the senior game and it gives them an opportunity to show what they can do. They must take their chance when it comes.

We also have some injuries right now, so it's important to rotate and keep the players as fresh as we can. But what I can say is very single player in our first-team squad is good enough to play for the club. If not, they would not be here. I trust all of them.

I want to welcome Wycombe to the Etihad Stadium this evening. They played a fantastic game on Saturday and have made a really, really good start to the season. When a team is winning, no matter what level they are playing at, it makes them dangerous because they have a good rhythm.

We will have to be very good this evening if we want to go to the next round.

They will provide us with a different challenge to RB Leipzig and Southampton and we need to be ready for that. I have watched their games and discussed their strengths with my players.

We are ready but make no mistake this will be a difficult night.

It's only three days since our last game. It is difficult to recover in such a short time, but we have tried to give the players as much rest as possible after two very demanding matches in two different competitions. One thing I know is that the attitude if my players is perfect. Every time I see them in training, it's always the same – they are happy, work hard and want to win. There is such desire in every single one of them, which as a manager is all you can ask.

I hope tonight is the start of another exciting journey in this competition. Enjoy the game and thank you, as always, for your support.

Manchester City 6, Wycombe Wanderers 1

Goals: De Bruyne (29), Mahrez (43, 83), Foden (46),
Torres (71), Palmer (88)

Line-up: Steffen, Egan-Riley, Mbete, Burns, Wilson-Esbrand (McAtee
72), Lavia, De Bruyne, Foden, Sterling, Mahrez, Torres (Palmer 72).
Subs not used: Carson, Dias, Jesus, Bernardo, Cancelo.

City came from behind to beat a spirited Wycombe
Wanderers 6-1 at the Etihad.

On a night when six teenagers made their first team
debut for City, there was plenty to entertain the Etihad
crowd with Wycombe more than playing their part.

First blood went to the Chairboys after the failure to
clear a corner was eventually punished when Brandon
Hanlan tapped into an empty net.

Their lead would only last six minutes, though, as
Kevin De Bruyne levelled before Josh Wilson-Esbarnd
marked his debut with an excellent assist for Riyad
Mahrez.

Phil Foden made it 3-1 with a thunderous left-foot
drive from 25 yards on the stroke of half time and
there was no let-up after the break as Foden sqaured for
Ferran Torres to finish cooly on 71 minutes.

Further strikes from Mahrez and Cole Palmer made
it 6-1 – a little harsh on the League One side but lapped
up nonetheless by the home fans.

Pep's post-match reaction: 'I know how special it is for our fans to see Academy players. We have talented players. We can count on them absolutely. They train with us every single day. They don't make bad faces; they don't make you feel uncomfortable in your decisions. They just have the desire to be something in world football. With their skills and desire – they got it at this club. I am so proud to be manager of this club. Today we saw a little bit of what they can do. We know exactly how good they are. As a manager I can enjoy it. I can use them. Without the incredible effort of many people in the Academy it would not be possible. We know they can do it. It is a dream for them to play in this kind of game in this stadium. We told them to do what they do. They will be supported. We have a really good generation of players. This is one of the nights I like to be manager. These young lads have just one desire, to play football. The priority in their life is to play football. Sometimes when you become a footballer, it is not the most important thing in your life. I was lucky to grow up in Barcelona. Won the Champions League with seven players from the Barca academy. That is unique. These young players feel grateful, their families are grateful for how many hours the club invested in them.'

Saturday, September 25
Premier League
Chelsea 0, Manchester City 1

Goal: Jesus (53)

*Line-up: Ederson, Walker, Dias, Laporte, Cancelo, Rodrigo,
Bernardo, Foden (Fernandinho 87), Grealish (Sterling 87),
De Bruyne (Mahrez 80), Jesus.
Subs not used: Steffen, Stones, Ake, Torres, Palmer, Lavia.*

City produced a fine display to beat Chelsea 1-0 at
Stamford Bridge and move up to second in the Premier
League table.

It was a performance full of graft and hard work, as
well as moments of wonderful attacking football.

Gabriel Jesus' deflected strike won it for City, who
thoroughly deserved the victory having dominated
proceedings and been by far the bolder team.

It was Pep Guardiola's 221st win as City boss – more
than any other manager in the Club's history.

*Pep's post-match reaction: 'I am so proud. What we have done
in these five years – players, backroom staff and all at the club –
working together to improve the club. It's an honour. Hopefully
we can make more [wins] and the next manager can come and
break the record. It means we have won many games. It's why*

we have won a lot of titles. In the last months we have done many good games otherwise you cannot win the Premier League and be runners-up in Champions League. It's incredible what these players have done. People say the Champions League was a disaster. We played 13 games, won 11, drew one and lost one. When this happens it is exceptional, that helps us and now we go to Paris to play. I have the feeling the players are there and want to do another good season for our people.'

Post-match notes

This win meant Pep Guardiola had now overseen more wins than any other manager in City's history. The victory was his 221st since taking charge in the summer of 2016, moving him ahead of Les McDowall, who secured 220 wins during his 13-year period as City boss, with one of his campaigns spent in the second tier.

Tuesday, September 28
UEFA Champions League
Paris Saint Germain 2, Manchester City 0

Line-up: Ederson, Walker, Cancelo, Dias, Laporte, Rodrigo, Bernardo, De Bruyne, Sterling (Jesus 78), Grealish (Foden 68), Mahrez. Subs not used: Steffen, Carson, Stones, Ake, Torres, Fernandinho, McAtee, Wilson-Esbrand.

A goal in each half for Paris Saint-Germain condemned City to a 2-0 defeat in the French capital.

Idrissa Gueye and Lionel Messi secured victory for the hosts who were forced to defend for large periods of the game.

City struck the bar twice in five seconds in the first period and had that gone in it would have likely been a different story.

Overall, City's stats were far better than PSG's – but the goals column is all that counts in games of fine margins such as this.

Pep's post-match reaction: 'I think we made a really good game, quite similar to Stamford Bridge. Maybe we were a little less aggressive in our first actions for the quality of the players that we have, but in general it was a fantastic game. We did everything, I didn't see the stats but I think we created enough

chances to score. Donnarumma was fantastic. The quality of
the players they have, we minimised for our game Neymar and
Messi being in contact with the ball and did not let Mbappe
run in behind but at the end 2-0, last ten minutes we were more
desperate with less control. The quality they have everyone knows
it, but I think we did a really good game with personality, but
we should've scored goals and we didn't do it and that's why
we lost the game. We dealt with PSG first of all. We know it's
impossible to control Leo all 90 minutes. Of course, he came
back from some injuries, which is why he needed a bit of rhythm
but we know him quite well and when he can run and be close
to the ball he's unstoppable. The way we have done is minimise
this as much as possible and create the chances that we could
create. We arrived here and played our game. They defended deep
with seven players, and it's always the risk if you lose the ball
and they can make one pass with Verratti who is an exceptional
player and they make contact with Neymar or Messi and run it's
always difficult.'

OCT

2021

After locking horns with Liverpool for the first time, our four seasons of Carabao Cup dominance came to an end, but our Champions League campaign got back on track with a superb showing in Bruges

3rd: Liverpool (PL) A
16th: Burnley (PL) H
19th: Club Bruges (CL) A
23rd: Brighton & Hove Albion (PL) A
27th: West Ham United (CC) A
30th: Crystal Palace (PL) H

Sunday, October 3
Premier League
Liverpool 2, Manchester City 2

Goals: Foden (69), De Bruyne (81)

Line-up: Ederson, Walker, Dias, Laporte, Cancelo, Rodrigo, De Bruyne, Bernardo, Grealish (Sterling 65), Jesus, Foden.
Subs not used: Steffen, Carson, Stones, Ake, Torres, Fernandinho, Mahrez, Palmer.

City twice came from behind to secure a draw at Liverpool in what was an enthralling Premier League encounter.

After dominating the first half, we then found ourselves behind after the break through Sadio Mane's 59th minute opener.

Man of the match Phil Foden then deservedly drew us level, only for Mo Salah to strike again for the hosts with 14 minutes left.

However, a superb Kevin De Bruyne effort nine minutes from time ensured that the spoils were shared in what was a classic clash between the sides.

Pep's post-match reaction: 'The Premier League is the best league in the world. Both teams wanted to win and wanted to try – it was pretty good. We compete and play with incredible personality, I'm very pleased with the way we played, the result we cannot change. The way we played in Stamford Bridge, Paris and here, shows we are a great team. When my team play that way three games – we cannot forget which team we played. Liverpool one of the best three teams in the world – you played with courage and personality like we have done – we played here at a good level. Today, we didn't lose but the draw is good, we just need to continue. I pray the players come back from international break safe. In the first half they didn't have one chance. But in the second half we knew it with their momentum, but how we reacted was brilliant. The last two times we've been here we played with huge personality. I'm so pleased with that. The way we played the first half and last 15 minutes was devastating and really good. After they went 1-0 up, Anfield changes a lot. But we stayed in the game and we came back twice and I am incredibly satisfied. It wasn't easy after coming back from Paris – the way we played the first half and then we are losing 1-0 and 2-1 – that doesn't give you the title but massive satisfaction. The way the team lose a game shows me we are a good team. And the way we lost in Paris and came back today. Overall we have started the season well. The game against Tottenham we were not together with half the squad on holiday and the worst game was against Southampton – the rest we were really good in all departments. Hopefully the players come back good from international break and move forward.'

On the rivalry with Liverpool...

For us it is an honour to have Liverpool as rivals. But

in many years we try to compete against this legendary club, for us it is an honour to be their rivals because it means we are there competing against one of the most historic teams in England.

They create gaps because of their movements. They create space in the middle and have high intensity in all places. It's very Jurgen.

If they win a lot of games it's because they are good. Not a lot of secrets. They won a Champions League and one Premier League.

All the time they are competing. I admire that. No matter what the situation, they try to play their game.

And Jurgen knows we are the same. We are who we are as a team. If it's going good, great, if it's going bad, improve.

v Burnley
Saturday, October 16

'ALL I ASK OF MY PLAYERS IS TO BE BRAVE AND TO PLAY OUR STYLE'

Premier League

Good afternoon, everyone and welcome back to the Etihad Stadium – it feels like a long time since our last game here against Wycombe and I am delighted we are back playing in front of our fans today. We like to travel together as a team and play matches away from home, but nothing can beat days like this at our stadium surrounded by our people.

A lot has happened since the Wycombe game. We played three times away from home against three top teams. The way we played over those three games was amazing. My players showed courage and personality in all of them, and I was so proud of the football we produced.

Since we arrived here, all I ask of my players is to be brave and to play our style. They did that in all of those matches, and it made me so happy. You cannot imagine how difficult it is to play Chelsea, PSG and Liverpool – all away – in the space of a week, but we did it and were so good.

Our last game, against Liverpool, showed everyone across the world why the Premier League is the best. It was incredible and a real privilege to be involved in a game like that.

Our focus this week has been on Burnley, a side who are always so difficult to play against. They have a very clear structure, they know their roles absolutely and they make it so hard for us. They are so physical and my players must be ready. Every time we have played Burnley during my time here, it has been difficult. We have watched footage of their games this season and we know exactly what to expect.

And today is a special one for us because four very important players from our past will receive medals for their part in our league title win back in 1968.

Bobby Kennedy, Stan Horne, Paul Hince and Harry Dowd.

Stan, Paul, Bobby and Harry all played a role in the history of Manchester City. They helped the Club win the league and it is so fitting that they are recognised.

I always say this club's history is so important. Without all the amazing people in the past who made this football club what it is today, we would not be here right now.

I want to send a huge congratulations to all the guys and their families – and I know our fans will give them a fantastic reception at the Etihad today.

And this match is also part of the Premier League's No Room for Racism campaign. This is a campaign everyone here at Manchester City supports. As people who love football we must do more to tackle discrimination, wherever it exists.

Thank you everyone for your support!

Manchester City 2, Burnley 0

Goals: Silva (12), De Bruyne (70)

*Line-up: Steffen, Cancelo, Stones, Laporte (Dias 72), Ake,
Rodrigo, De Bruyne (Fernandinho 83), Bernardo (Palmer 90),
Mahrez, Foden, Sterling.
Subs not used: Carson, Slicker, Walker, Gundogan, Grealish, Zinchenko.*

Goals from Bernardo Silva and Kevin De Bruyne gave Manchester City a deserved victory over Burnley at the Etihad Stadium.

Pep Guardiola's side were superior throughout the contest and opened the scoring in the 12th minute when Nick Pope pushed Phil Foden's drive from the edge of the area into the path of Bernardo, who lashed home from two yards.

The Clarets had lost 5-0 on each of their last four visits to the Etihad, and the early goal suggested we might record another convincing victory, but our trademark cutting edge deserted us until De Bruyne struck 20 minutes from time.

City had seen several chances go begging up until that point, but the Belgian made no mistake when the visitors failed to clear his initial cross, latching onto the loose ball to rifle a first-time finish into the far corner off his left foot.

It sealed a well-earned three points for the defending Premier League champions, who were on the front foot from the off.

Pep's post-match reaction: 'My players always play well because they give everything and they did it in a difficult game after the international break. Their team is always organised. You have to adjust and adapt. I am so satisfied with the way we played. Bernardo is in incredibly good form alongside Rodri. Both played incredibly well the last four or five games. He is at the level of the second season when we won 98 points and he was out of this world. He is at the same level. He is so intuitive; he always gives us the extra ball that we need. Today he scored a goal, that's important for him. The performance of Bernardo has been extraordinary again. He is so generous and the effort and the way he plays is fantastic. We are so lucky to have him. He was an incredible signing for us. All I want is his happiness. He deserves the best. He is a joy to have as manager. When he doesn't play he always tries to do his best. He is at his best level right now.'

Post-match notes

This was Fernandinho's 250th Premier League appearance. He is only the second Brazilian, after Willian, to reach that milestone.

Tuesday, October 19
UEFA Champions League
Club Bruges 1, Manchester City 5

Goals: Cancelo (30), Mahrez (43, 84), Walker (53), Palmer (67)

Line-up: Ederson, Walker, Cancelo, Dias, Laporte (Ake 57), Rodrigo
(Fernandinho 71), De Bruyne (Palmer 65), Bernardo (Gundogan 57),
Grealish, Mahrez, Foden (Sterling 65).
Subs not used: Steffen, Carson, Jesus, Zinchenko.

City bounced back from the Group A loss to Paris Saint-Germain with a superb performance against Club Brugge.

City were magnificent from start to finish, with the 5-1 victory – if anything – flattering the hosts.

The scoreline equalled our biggest winning margin in a Champions League away game, having beaten Basel and Feyenoord 4-0 – though this is the first time we've hit five goals away from home in the Champions League proper.

Joao Cancelo opened the scoring, with Riyad Mahrez doubling the lead before the break.

Kyle Walker and Cole Palmer added further strikes in the second-half before Brugge pulled back a barely deserved consolation.

Mahrez then bagged his second of the night a few minutes later to restore order.

Pep's post-match reaction: 'It was a great performance apart from the last 10 minutes of the first half and the last 10 minutes of the second. We played really good, had total control, creating chances and I am so satisfied with the way we played. Normally when you win that way it is easy, but I know what they did here against PSG and won in Leipzig – one of the toughest teams in Germany so I'm not going to underestimate their team – what we have done we thoroughly deserve it. It was one of the best performances we have done in Europe. I am not going to underestimate Brugge. I know them quite well. I spoke with Vincent Kompany and he gave me some info. He knows Brugge better than me. He said be careful in the final third, they have a fast central defender, especially the left one. I think we made a really good performance in many aspects so they could not be who they are. I know perfectly well who they are. I looked over Brugge during the international break. I looked at many games. I know how good they did against PSG. It is a few weeks before they travel to Manchester, and I am pretty sure they are going to adjust. It will not be the same, that's for sure. They have pride, they will see the game, see what they can do better. We will have to prepare as best as possible to take all the points. We made a good game, our pressing was good. We recovered the ball so quickly and after that we used the ball with a lot of sense. All of us are delighted with the performance we have done.'

Saturday, October 23
Premier League
Brighton & Hove Albion 1, Manchester City 4

Goals: Gundogan (13), Foden (28, 31), Mahrez (95)

Line-up: Ederson, Walker, Dias, Laporte, Cancelo, Rodrigo,
Gundogan (Fernandinho 75), Bernardo, Grealish (De Bruyne 77),
Jesus (Mahrez 86), Foden.
Subs not used: Steffen, Stones, Ake, Zinchenko,
Edozie, Palmer.

Manchester City produced a spectacular performance to beat Brighton 4-1 at the AMEX Stadium and move up to second in the Premier League table.

All the hallmarks of Pep Guardiola's tenure were on display, with intense hard-work and tenacity coupled with outstanding attacking quality.

First-half goals from Ilkay Gundogan and two from Phil Foden put City in total control.

An Alexis Mac Allister penalty with 10 minutes remaining cut the arrears, but Riyad Mahrez's expert finish in injury time sealed a ninth win in our last 12 matches across all competitions (W9, D2, L1).

Pep's post-match reaction: 'Some players play in one position, some play football. Phil (Foden) in dropped positions is maybe more dangerous because he is so young, but he has the quality to play in the final third. He can play striker, false nine, winger right and left. In the last games he has many chances and in front of keeper didn't take right decisions because is young but I am more than pleased with the performances he has given. I like him as a player. He gives us things we need at a times. He has quality to play this role. At Anfield he played as a winger and was our important player. He is a midfield player with a lot of sense for goals, the only thing for Phil is to be calm on and off the pitch, because he is still young. I will tell you the reason why we didn't play well in half an hour of the second half. In this game, you have to have the ball. If you don't have it, you suffer. Brighton know what to do. We suffered together and it is a good lesson for the future. It doesn't matter what stadium, the only time you have success is to play with the ball – to have the ball. We gave the ball away and when the opponent is good, you suffer.'

Post-match notes

Ilkay Gundogan had now scored a goal in each of his three Premier League appearances at Brighton – Jamie Vardy (4) is the only away player to score more Premier League goals at the Amex Community Stadium.

Wednesday, October 27
Carabao Cup
West Ham United 0, Manchester City 0
(West Ham win 5-3 on penalties)

Line-up: Steffen, Walker (Cancelo 46), Stones, Ake, Zinchenko, Fernandinho, Gundogan, De Bruyne (Grealish 81), Mahrez (Foden 72), Palmer (Jesus 76), Sterling.
Subs not used: Carson, Dias, Laporte, Rodrigo, Edozie.

Manchester City's four seasons of Carabao Cup dominance came to an end after a penalty shootout defeat to West Ham United saw the defending champions bow out in the fourth round.

After a goalless, but entertaining 90 minutes in which Pep Guardiola's men were superior, the Hammers prevailed on spot-kicks after Phil Foden dragged his opening effort wide of the right post.

David Moyes' side held their nerve to successfully convert all five of their attempts to seal a 5-3 shootout victory, as City lost a League Cup tie for the first time since October 2016.

Pep's post-match reaction: 'An incredible run has finished (but) we finished in a good way. We played in a really good way, creating chances against a team who defended deep. On penalties they were better. Congratulations to West Ham. Next year we will be back. One of the toughest games we played at home when one side was better than us last season was West Ham They're doing well in the Premier League and the Europa League and now they are in the quarter-finals of the Carabao Cup. (They are a) fantastic team, (and have a) fantastic manager. We knew it. We did our game. I didn't see the stats, but I thought we did a good game. Sometimes it happens. Next season we will be back.'

On the secret of his longevity...

I could not be in a better place right now. I have everything I need to do my job as good as possible.

[I am] surrounded by fantastic players. Sometimes players are sad because they are not playing but I have incredible staff who support me unconditionally.

I have to find solutions to improve the team. This club remains so stable in many things, and I'm sure the next step, when I will be replaced, the manager will do an exceptional job because the bases are there.

v Crystal Palace
Saturday, October 30

'I HAVE BEEN SO IMPRESSED WITH MY PLAYERS – THEY'RE FOCUSED AND HUNGRY'

Premier League

Hello everyone and welcome to the Etihad Stadium. It's been two weeks since we were last here and, as always, it's great to back playing with our people here to support us.

Firstly, I want to say how delighted we all are to hear that Guido De Pauw is stable and recovering after being attacked following our Champions League win in Brugge. It has made me so proud to see our football club come together in support of Guido. The players wanted to show their support last week at Brighton by wearing t-shirts – and those fans who travelled with us to the AMEX brought a banner to make it clear to Guido and his family we are all willing him to recover.

We know how much Guido has given to this football club over the years with passion and support and this has been our time to give something back to him.

Out thoughts are still with him and his family, and we all hope he can make a full recovery. It would be so good to see him back here at the Etihad at some stage in the future. He and his family would be so welcome.

I thought we were excellent at Brighton. I have been so impressed with my players in recent weeks, and the game we played on Saturday was a continuation of what I have been seeing. This squad is focused and hungry, and I love watching them play.

And it was the same against West Ham. The result was not what we wanted, and our incredible four-year run was ended, but I could not fault my players for the effort, spirit and quality they showed. We created so many chances against a team who defend so well, but it wasn't to be. Huge congratulations to West Ham and, of course, we will be back next year trying to win that competition again.

Today we face Crystal Palace, and I am especially delighted to welcome Patrick Vieira to the Etihad. As a player, he reached the very top of the game – he won absolutely everything and was always a leader in whichever side he played in. Everyone in football respects and admires him for what he achieved and the way he conducted himself throughout his career.

And everyone who remembers Patrick from his time at City tells me what an amazing impact he had and what a top professional he was. He came here to help Manchester City become winners and he did that. I have no doubts he is going to be a success at Crystal Palace. That's why I know today's game will be really tough. Patrick's teams play good football, and my players must be ready to be at their best. We have analysed them this week and I have made sure the players know what they will be coming up against. It should be a fantastic match.

Thank you, as always, for your continued support. We love and appreciate you and we could not do our jobs without you alongside us. Enjoy the game.

Manchester City 0, Crystal Palace 2

*Line-up: Ederson, Walker, Cancelo (Mahrez 77), Dias,
Laporte, Rodrigo, De Bruyne (Stones 60), Bernardo, Grealish
(Sterling77), Jesus, Foden.
Subs not used: Steffen, Ake, Gundogan, Zinchenko, Fernandinho,
Palmer.*

City's unbeaten home run came to an end against
Crystal Palace.

City were on the back-foot after conceding inside the
first 10 minutes, and after losing Aymeric Laporte to
a straight red in first-half added time, faced an uphill
struggle thereafter.

Despite a stirring second-half and and a goal
disallowed by VAR, Palace snatched a late second to
record a controversial 2-0 victory.

*Pep's post-match reaction: 'We conceded early on – how many
chances did they have after their goal? It was quite similar to
when Palace came here last year with Roy Hodgson with 10
men back – we lost one game one year, drew another one. The
same process – the keeper takes time, the rhythm, the momentum,
long balls to Zaha and they are so good at keeping the ball.
They have quality and they defend really, really well with
solidarity, defending the gaps and stopping us from shooting and
I cannot say we had many but in the first half, we had chances*

to score, but when we went to 10 men it was more difficult, we scored but VAR disallowed it and even Rodri had one or two chances to score but in the end they counter-attack and scored a second goal. But when you play 50 minutes 10 against 11, it is difficult for a team like us because you need the process and to do everything right. The players showed character and tried, but unfortunately many, many things went wrong and we lost the game. They have very good players. When they get the ball, they keep it and want to play. I said after the Brighton game to prepare mentally straight away because it would be very difficult. I saw against Brighton and Arsenal so I knew perfectly how difficult they are and they showed it today.'

NOV

2021

With five wins out of five for the month,
City were now purring along, making
light work of a trip to Old Trafford and
qualifying for the knock-out stages of the
Champions League for the ninth straight
season, and in doing so topping our group
for the fifth season in a row

3rd: Club Bruges (CL) H
6th: Manchester United (PL) A
21st: Everton (PL) H
24th: Paris Saint Germain (CL) H
28th: West Ham (PL) H

November 2021

v Club Bruges
Wednesday, November 3

'QUALIFYING FOR THE LAST 16 IS DIFFICULT BUT WE MUST BE ABLE TO HANDLE THE PRESSURE'

UEFA Champions League

GOOD evening, everyone. and welcome back to the Etihad Stadium. It's good to see you all here so soon after the game against Crystal Palace.

Looking back to the game with Crystal Palace, we were obviously very disappointed to lose.

For 25-30 minutes of the second half we were good, but when you play for 50 minutes with 10 men against 11, it is difficult. The players showed character and tried, but we lost the game.

We know Palace have a very good team. I said to the players after the Brighton game to prepare mentally because it would be very difficult – I know perfectly how difficult they are.

It was my 200th Premier League game as City manager and I can honestly say I have loved every single one. I am so incredibly happy here. I am supported perfectly by everyone who works in this organisation, and I have been able to watch this team grow and grow over my time here.

I could not be more satisfied, and I will do everything I can to make sure we continue progressing. I am a lucky guy to work for Manchester City and lead this amazing group of players.

Tonight, it's back to the Champions League as we welcome Club Brugge to our stadium. It will be a pleasure to face them. They are Belgian champions, and although we won the away game two weeks ago, I saw enough to know they have quality and can hurt us.

We saw what they did against PSG, and they won in Leipzig – one of the toughest teams in Germany. I am not going to underestimate them, and my players will be absolutely ready. I was so satisfied with the way we played in Brugge and I want to see the same qualities from the team again this evening.

We know if we win tonight, it will be a huge step forward for us in this group. As I say every single season, the quality in the Champions League is so high now that qualifying for the last 16 is incredibly difficult. This brings huge pressure, but I love pressure, it's a huge part of being a manager, and my players must handle it too.

A big thank you, as always, to you guys. Your support drives the team on and makes a huge difference.

Enjoy today's game!

Manchester City 4, Club Bruges 1

Goals: Foden (15), Mahrez (54), Sterling (72), Jesus (92)

Line-up: Ederson, Walker (Zinchenko 78), Cancelo, Stones, Laporte, Rodrigo, Gundogan, Bernardo (De Bruyne 75) , Grealish (Jesus 68), Foden (Palmer 79), Mahrez (Sterling 68).
Subs not used: Steffen, Carson, Dias, Aké, Fernandinho.

Second half goals from Riyad Mahrez, Raheem Sterling and Gabriel Jesus helped City secure a deserved 4-1 Champions League group win over Club Brugge at the Etihad.

In a fast-paced and entertaining clash, Phil Foden's early first half opener had been cancelled by a John Stones own goal, with the Belgian side proving dangerous opponents.

But Pep Guardiola's side stepped up the attacking ante after the break and goals from Mahrez and substitutes Sterling – his first in Europe in 13 months – and Jesus were no more than we deserved.

The victory – our second in successive games against Brugge – also moved us top of Group A, leaving us in the driving seat to clinch a last 16 place with City knowing a point over Paris Saint-Germain later this month would seal the deal.

Pep's post-match reaction: 'The second half was really good. A good game, good victory. The message is easy for the players that every game is so important. Every game my focus is the next one, and I never think about the second one. I know the game against United is the most important thing, we are going to create a good environment but you cannot imagine how important today was. We have done two fantastic games and now we think about United. I know how good they are – we saw it last season and they have one of the best players in history, a scoring machine who can do unique things. Of course we have a plan and we are going to try to do our own thing. We play our way and that is what we do.'

Saturday, November 6
Premier League
Manchester United 0, Manchester City 2

Goals: Bailly (7 og), Silva (45)

Line-up: Ederson, Walker, Dias, Stones, Cancelo, Rodrigo, Gundogan, Bernardo, De Bruyne, Jesus, Foden.
Subs not used: Steffen, Carson, Ake, Sterling, Grealish, Zinchenko, Fernandinho, Mahrez, Palmer.

City produced a flawless performance in the 186th Manchester Derby, comfortably beating United 2-0 at Old Trafford to move up to second in the Premier League table for the time being at least.

Eric Bailly's own goal gave City an early lead and Bernardo Silva's backpost tap-in, which brought a 26-pass move to a conclusion, doubled our advantage just before half time.

The second half was a masterclass in possession football as City toyed with United to see the game out comfortably and earn a vital three points.

Pep's post-match reaction: 'We spoke about the fact they are a transition team. We had to put the ball in the fridge – a lot of passes and at the last moments arrive. Except ten mins in the second half, the rest was really good. The commitment and the fact is we played a really good game from beginning to the end. The best way to silence Old Trafford is to have the ball…have the ball and we did it. And we played a really good game except for ten minutes in the second half where we missed some ball. For our fans, Manchester City is the best club in Manchester, for United red is the best. All we can say is that in the last years we have done really well, winning a lot of titles and being there all the time. There have been other games like when we could be champions at the Etihad in 2018 when we were 2-0 up at half time and lost 3-2, in the first half maybe it was 4 or 5 and we lost 3-2, the second half we were not good. Some games we were good but not for as much longer like Saturday was, it's the game where we controlled (things) more specifically. We know each other better, we know the opponent better, and we need the ball to play good. We have the desire when we don't have it to recover it and after that play and play and play. Not to attack quicker you will score more goals, just to arrive in the right tempo, I love to arrive in the boxes, not be in the boxes. The way we play with a lot of passes, we are able to have Gabby, Bernardo, Phil and Kevin who can arrive and surprise the opponent. On Saturday we did it really well. I know these games are important. Before we have to prepare and be calm, not too many emotions to prepare the game. But afterwards when you have success, or you play good and win the game after that you have to celebrate it with your City neighbours. It makes me so proud.'

All three of Bernardo Silva's goals against Manchester United for Manchester City have come at Old Trafford, scoring in three of his last four appearances there – he has only netted more goals against Burnley (four) in his time at Man City.

On the way his players have played so far this season...

I have the feeling we are there but we know how demanding it is – we dropped points against Southampton, who played really well, lost to Crystal Palace. This is the Premier League.

You see the teams right now at the bottom of the league, you say: 'How difficult is it to beat them?!'

That's why it's step by step, game by game – not thinking about runs of victories. We won the last one, try to win the next one, then go to PSG and West Ham,

Every game, have the intention to do a good game and be ourselves. We have done it this season. I said one month ago: in important games, we have played better than we have done together in six season in terms of control and many things.

To win the Premier League you have to be a machine – consistent every three days in every game – and this is the challenge.

Pep Guardiola

v Everton
Sunday, November 21

'IF WE CONTINUE TO PLAY WITH PERSONALITY AND CHARACTER, THEN I'M SURE WE CAN HAVE A GOOD SEASON'

Premier League

GOOD afternoon and welcome back to the Etihad Stadium. It's a pleasure to have you here with us for this game against Everton, a side full of quality. It should be a really good game against them.

As I always say, it's a pleasure to face the best managers and Rafa Benitez is fantastic. What he has achieved in the game – at Valencia and Liverpool, in particular – has been amazing. Tactically, he is so clever, and his teams are always so well organised and difficult to beat.

Everton are a side with a lot of weapons, believe me. They have pace, physicality and have players with individual quality. You will see today how tough they are.

Like we do for every game, myself and the players have been preparing for the game, and we know exactly what we can expect. We must be ready and at our best.

I want to send a warm welcome to Rafa and all the Everton players and fans. I hope you enjoy your day here at the Etihad.

It's been a while since our last game, but it was a memorable one! Always when you win a derby, it is a special day – but the way we played at Old Trafford is what we pleased me most. I said after the game, but I want to say it again: I have so much admiration and respect for these players for their approach to the game. Always we play our style, no matter who we are facing. That makes me so happy because, as a manager, that is all I ask. The players are incredibly committed to this football club and our way of playing, and that is why we played such a good game from beginning to end at Old Trafford. The best way to win against Manchester United, who are so good on the counter, is to have the ball and we did that really well.

I hope we can continue playing in this way, with personality and character. If we do that, I am confident we can have a good season.

It is a pleasure being the Manchester City manager. I love our fans, I love my players and I am supported absolutely perfectly by everyone at the club.

I want to say thank you for the continued support.

Enjoy today's game!

Manchester City 3, Everton 0

Goals: Sterling (44), Rodrigo (55), Silva (86)

Line-up: Ederson, Walker, Stones, Laporte (Ake 76), Cancelo, Rodrigo, Gundogan, Bernardo, Palmer (McAtee 87), Foden (Mahrez 57), Sterling.
Subs not used: Steffen, Carson, Dias, Jesus, Zichenko, Fernandinho.

Rodrigo scored a goal of the season contender as Manchester City beat Everton 3-0 in a one-sided affair at the Etihad Stadium.

The Spaniard beat Jordan Pickford with a 25-yard thunderbolt to double City's lead after Raheem Sterling converted Joao Cancelo's superb cross to mark his 300th

Premier League appearance with a goal.

Bernardo Silva wrapped up the three points late on, when he reacted quickest to slide Cole Palmer's deflected strike through Pickford's legs from six-yards.

It was another masterful performance from the defending champions, who replicated the dominant display against Manchester United a fortnight ago to claim a deserved victory.

Pep's post-match reaction: 'It was good before the international break and it was good after the break. Rafa is a master of the moments defensively, with a team that doesn't want to attack, just defend, defend, defend and wait for the counter attack with Gray and Richarlison. We made a lot of passes and at the right moment attacked them and when we lost the ball were good in transition. We handled the moments in the game. I'm so satisfied with the performance after the international break. We were really good and I'm very pleased. We knew, the last time we played against Rafa with Newcastle, we always struggled a lot. We won by a small margin. That's why it was so difficult. We knew they could play four or five at the back. That's why it is important to move a lot. Today we were better, we conceded few, we waited for the right moments. That's why I am very pleased. The performance was really good. We now focus on Wednesday and then after that, West Ham. We don't stop and we will see our level at the end of the season. We have a tough calendar. We are not top but we are not far away.'

Pep Guardiola

'TO MAKE IT TO THE NEXT PHASE OF THE CHAMPIONS LEAGUE WOULD BE A FANTASTIC ACHIEVEMENT'

UEFA Champions League

Good evening, everyone, and welcome to the Etihad Stadium for what should be an amazing night of football.

The Champions League is a wonderful competition, and we are playing one of the best sides in the world, here in our beautiful stadium in front of our people. What more could we ask for?

These are the kind of games those of us who love football want to experience and it's a pleasure and a privilege to be involved in them.

I want to welcome Mauricio and all the PSG players and staff to our stadium this evening. It should be a fantastic match. We saw in the first game in Paris – and in last season's semi-final matches – what a brilliant team PSG are, and I am sure they will come here tonight to try and win the game.

I say this every season, but the Champions League is now of such high quality that qualifying for the last-16 is a fantastic achievement. We can do that tonight and, if we can make it to the next phase, it will be because we are one of Europe's best 16 teams. That is our target.

Watching my side on Sunday against Everton was a pleasure. I thought we played a really impressive game. We knew from the times we played against Rafa when he was at Newcastle that it would be tough. Always his sides make it hard, so to win the way we did was very pleasing.

We kept the ball brilliantly. At the right moments we

attacked them and when we lost the ball were good in transition. We handled the important moments in the game really well. I was so satisfied.

Our performance before the international break was excellent and our first performance after the international break was excellent, which is a good sign and I have to give my players credit. Their schedule is not easy, but they are always so professional and they give everything for Manchester City.

I also want to thank our fans. You guys were top on Sunday and it helped us so much. Thank you, it means a lot to the players, my staff and to me.

We have such a tough calendar. I want my team to keep going, keep fighting, and at the end of the season let's see where we are.

As always, I am only focusing on the next game. So, since Sunday, it has been PSG. After tonight, I look at West Ham. Never, ever in my life have I jumped ahead even one game. The most important match is always the next one and that's how we will continue to approach things.

Enjoy tonight's game!

Manchester City 2, Paris Saint Germain 1

Goals: Sterling (63), Jesus (76)

Line-up: Ederson, Walker, Dias, Stones, Zinchenko (Jesus 54), Rodrigo, Cancelo, Gundogan, Bernardo, Sterling, Mahrez.
Subs not used: Steffen, Carson, Ake, Laporte, Fernandinho, Palmer, McAtee.

Second half goals from Raheem Sterling and Gabriel Jesus fired City to a deserved Champions League win over Paris Saint-Germain and sealed our ticket into the last 16.

In what was a pulsating Etihad encounter, Kylian Mbappe had fired the visitors into a 50th minute lead against the run of play.

But, roared on by a passionate crowd, Sterling struck to level affairs on 63 minutes before substitute Jesus rounded off a memorable night by converting from close range 14 minutes from time to seal the deal.

Pep's post-match reaction: 'Of course, PSG, what a team, what players, what could I say. Performance is quite similar to Paris a month ago. Today we created more chances in the first half. We pressed really well in Paris and we adjusted because we learnt what we do. They decided not to play with Di Maria, but they are so dangerous. They have good players so you can lose a game like this. They quality they have…we did so well. We were aggressive without the ball. We defended well. We did it. We played really well. In football the results are random. Nobody knows what will happen. What gives you consistency is how you perform and the way we are performing is really good. The people enjoy watching and hopefully we can sustain this for as long as possible. The players come back from injury and hopefully help us do it. They have a lot of quality, we tried to defend away from our goal because they can do anything. Except for the five minutes after our goal when they counter-attacked but could not finish because Ruben defended really well, so I say congratulations to everyone at our Club. We are into last 16 and will try our best in February to go to quarter-finals.'

Post-match notes

This is the ninth straight season that City have qualified for the Champions League knockout stages. It is also the fifth successive season we have finished top of our group with City only the second English side to achieve that feat after Manchester United.

On how City will be his one and only English club...

I would love, I said many times, when I finish here, the pleasure to lead a team at a World Cup. But it is not easy to find it. There are only a few positions.

I would like it but if it doesn't happen I will train clubs, so it will not be a problem.

But in England, being here I think always I will be Man City and if I have to come back it would be at Man City, if they want me. I would not train another club in England apart from this club.

I want to be here [at City] as long as possible, as much as my energy and love is here. After that I don't know what will happen.

November 2021

v West Ham United
Sunday, November 28

'I WANT TO SEE HUNGER AND DESIRE FROM MY PLAYERS – JUST LIKE I HAVE DONE THROUGHOUT THE SEASON'

Premier League

Hello everyone. Welcome back to the Etihad. It's the third time in eight days we have been here together, and I can honestly say there's nothing I enjoy more than being in our stadium with our people supporting us.

The atmosphere on Wednesday was fantastic. Thank you for making it such a special night. It's one I will never forget.

To beat PSG, with the quality they possess, and finish top of such a difficult group with one game left, is fantastic. I am honestly really, really proud of my players. We played a good game against a top team. We were so aggressive when we lost the ball, we defended well and produced quality in the box.

But the most important thing is we have made it through. To be in the last 16 of the Champions League again really is a fantastic achievement for this football club. It's the ninth year in a row this club has reached the knockout stages, which says everything about the strength of this organisation.

The Champions League is an incredible competition and to always be there, in the last 16, can only happen if everyone is working hard and pushing in the same direction. I want to thank everyone at the club for their support and hard work because without them, it would not be possible.

We will now do our best in February to make it to the quarter final. But now it's back to the Premier League and I want to extend a warm welcome to the West Ham fans and players. I am expecting this to be a really entertaining game.

It is a pleasure to welcome David Moyes here today – he is a person I have so much respect for. The job he has done at West Ham has been exceptional and he deserves all the praise he is getting right now. Of course, it is no surprise after what he did at Everton over such a long period, but the way he has turned West Ham into such a consistent team really has been impressive.

This will be another incredibly tough game. We must be aggressive with the ball and fight to win it back if we lose it. I want to see hunger and desire from my players – just like I have throughout this season so far.

Thank you for being here and enjoy the game.

Manchester City 2, West Ham United 1

Goals: Gundogan (33), Fernandinho (90)

Line-up: Ederson, Walker, Cancelo, Laporte, Dias, Rodrigo, Gundogan, Bernardo, Sterling (Fernandinho 87), Jesus, Mahrez.
Subs not used: Steffen, Carson, Stones, Zinchenko, Ake, Palmer, McAtee.

City had to battle a dogged West Ham and blizzard conditions to edge a narrow 2-1 victory at the Etihad.

In freezing temperatures, Ilkay Gundogan gave City a first-half lead after good work by Riyad Mahrez.

And though chances came and went for the champions,

sub Fernandinho's 90th-minute goal proved vital, with Manuel Lanzini pulling one back in added time.

Pep's post-match reaction: 'The groundskeepers, the guys who take care of the pitch, were the men of the match today. They did an incredible job for us to be able to play the game today. We came from a tough game in midweek against PSG and we know exactly which team we face today. The amount of chances we created in the first half, in the conditions that we played, [it's] a huge victory for us, for the effort for the players, for the performance in general. We didn't concede much, we controlled the counter attack. Maybe we could have found another rhythm but the weather didn't allow us to do it. A good performance from all of us.'

Post-match notes

It wasn't quite a repeat of our famous 'Ballet on Ice' against Tottenham in 1967, but as far as the conditions went, it was very similar. That day in December at Maine Road, City gracefully swept aside Spurs 4-1 with Tony Book's secret tip of unscrewing the studs on the boots giving the Blues a sure-footed confidence that resulted in a masterful display by Joe Mercer's men. That sort of boot doesn't exists 50-plus years on, but the skill and technique of the current City players was commendable in the winter wonderland of a pitch at the Etihad. And the three points will have warmed the freezing supporters on this most wintry afternoon in East Manchester.

DEC

2021

A busy month saw us set new records for wins and goals scored in a calendar year as we once again went through the Premier League without dropping points, with both Raheem Sterling and Ederson reaching significant personal milestones

1st: Aston Villa (PL) A
4th: Watford (PL) A
7th: RB Leipzig (CL) A
11th: Wolverhampton Wanderers (PL) H
14th: Leeds (PL) H
19th: Newcastle (PL) A
26th: Leicester City (PL) H
29th: Brentford (PL) A

Wednesday, December 1
Premier League
Aston Villa 1, Manchester City 2

Goals: Dias (27), Silva (43)

Line-up: Ederson, Cancelo, Dias, Ake, Zinchenko, Fernandinho,
Rodrigo, Bernardo, Sterling, Jesus (Grealish 87), Mahrez.
Subs not used: Steffen, Carson, Mbete, Foden, Palmer,
McAtee, Lavia, Wilson-Esbrand.

Stunning first half goals from Ruben Dias and Bernardo were enough to earn depleted City a crucial 2-1 Premier League win at Aston Villa.

Despite being shorn of several key players through injury, illness and suspension, Pep Guardiola's reigning champions produced a sumptuous opening 45 minutes at Villa Park capped off by quite superb goals from Portuguese duo Dias and Silva.

A 47th minute effort from Villa's Ollie Watkins made for a hard-fought second half.

However, City held firm to deservedly seal our 10th league win of the season and so stay hot on the heels of leaders Chelsea.

It was also Pep Guardiola's 150th Premier League win.

The City boss is only the fourth manager to achieve

the feat and he achieved it in 204 games – quicker time that Sir Alex Ferguson who hit 150 wins in 247 games.

Pep's post-match reaction: 'The game we played was fantastic. It was a difficult game. We knew it. I understand why. Especially after conceding early in the second half, the way we reacted... we played really well. Bernardo scored a fantastic goal. When a player has this quality it depends on them. He is a player on another level. Ruben has good personalities. He scored a really good goal. I'm quite proud yeah (to make it 150 Premier League victories). It means we have won some games! I didn't know, they have told me in the flash interview. It's a lot in the Premier League and we did it in a short time and it means what we have these years is all together. A big compliment for the whole club, the chairman and there is more to come.'

Post-match notes

There is something about Wednesday nights that seems to bring the very best out of City. Incredibly, this was our 16th consecutive Wednesday night win in the Premier League – a remarkable run that stretches all the way back to Boxing Day 2018.

Saturday, December 4
Premier League
Watford 1, Manchester City 3

Goals: Sterling (4), Silva (31, 63)

Line-up: Ederson, Walker, Cancelo, Dias, Laporte, Rodrigo,
Gundogan (De Bruyne 67), Bernardo,
Grealish (Mahrez 68), Foden (Jesus 75), Sterling.
Subs not used: Steffen, Carson, Stones, Ake, Zinchenko, Fernandinho.

City climbed to the top of the Premier League for the first time this season after beating Watford 3-1 at Vicarage Road.

It was yet another scintillating performance on the road as City also set a new Club record in the process.

Goals from Raheem Sterling and Bernardo gave the champions a two-goal advantage at the break, though it perhaps could and should have been many more.

It was a similar story after the re-start, with Bernardo scoring a sumptuous third to seal victory just past the hour.

Phil Foden and Jack Grealish hit the woodwork before Chucho Hernandez pulled one back on 74 minutes.

Pep's post-match reaction: 'Everyone is back, it doesn't matter who plays, we are consistent and winning games but in football everything goes down in one second. More than pleased with what the guys have done in this tough period and now comes the toughest one for amount of games, weather, injuries. We keep going with this rhythm and try to play good. We created more chances than Wednesday, but the game could be over after 15 minutes. The most important thing is that we won. We played in a consistent way, controlled, we played a good game again. Take a look at what happened with Manchester United and Chelsea (at Vicarage Road). We played really well, we didn't allow them to be who they are. I have a lot of respect for Claudio, but it's not that Watford didn't want to do it – we didn't allow it. We missed a lot of chances and hopefully next time, we can convert. Scoring goals is the most difficult thing in football and we're not specialists but we're playing well and it's important to create the chances. There's many games to come and it's the toughest part of the season. We'll try to continue at this level and this rhythm.'

Post-match notes

The 3-1 win over Watford means City set a new Club record for top-flight league victories in a calendar year. It was our 31st league win in 2021, surpassing the previous record of 30 set in both 2017 and 2019.

Tuesday, December 7
UEFA Champions League
RB Leipzig 2, Manchester City 1

Goal: Mahrez (76)

Line-up: Steffen, Walker, Stones, Ake (Dias 86),
Zinchenko, Fernandinho, Gundogan, De Bruyne (Palmer 86),
Grealish, Foden (Foden 45), Mahrez.
Subs not used: Ederson, Carson, Egan-Riley, McAtee,
Lavia, Wilson-Esbrand.

Ten-man City's Champions League Group A campaign ended on a frustrating note as Pep Guardiola's side slipped to a 2-1 defeat away to RB Leipzig.

Though we were already assured of top spot and a place in the last-16 draw, a City side showing seven changes from the team that won at Watford on Saturday, strove to try and end the group stage on a winning note.

However Dominik Szoboszlai and Andre Silva struck in both halves to power a fired-up Leipzig into a two-goal lead.

Though Riyad Mahrez set up a grandstand finish with a fine stooping header on 76 minutes, City couldn't force a leveller. And the match ended with Kyle Walker being sent off for foul play nine minutes from time to seal a disappointing night in eastern Germany.

Pep's post-match reaction: 'We played better in the second half, more aggressive, we played to win the game and we lost it so congratulations to Leipzig. In the first half we lacked rhythm, we had problems to contact and they had a really good team, we knew before group stage but second half much better. Unfortunately we were punished with one or two mistakes. We made an incredible group stage. We qualified with a game left in a top group, so we are more than satisfied with the performance in every single game. Of course, it's better to not concede goals, but the way we played all the games we played much better than the opponent except today in the first half. In general, we made an incredible group stage. In February hopefully we can arrive in the best condition possible.'

v Wolves
Saturday, December 11

'I COMPLETELY TRUST MY PLAYERS AND I KNOW HOW HARD THEY WORK TO BRING SUCCESS TO THIS CLUB'

Premier League

Welcome everyone to the Etihad Stadium. I want to start by sending my condolences to the family and friends of Mr Ian Niven MBE who sadly passed away last week. Mr Niven was a member of the board here at Manchester City for almost 25 years and then became an honorary president until his passing. He was someone committed to City and without people like him, this club would not be what it is today.

He lived an extraordinary life, serving his country during World War II, and it is a real pleasure to know he was still attending City matches until his passing last week. He deserves so much respect for what he achieved in his life and his dedication to this club.

I also want to take some time to reflect on our Champions League campaign so far. We made an incredible group stage, and we should be proud. Before we started, we knew we had a really difficult group, but we finished top with a game left to play, which is a fantastic effort from everybody. So congratulations to my players, my staff and everyone at Manchester City because to be there in the best 16 teams in Europe once again is amazing for this football club.

On Monday, we find out who we will face in the last 16. No matter who we get in the draw, it will be a beautiful occasion. Only the very best teams are still there and let's see if we can arrive at that stage in our best condition possible. If we do, we will have a good chance of going through to the quarter-finals.

I trust my players completely and I know how hard they work every day to bring success to Manchester City. As I have said many times, it is a privilege to manage this squad – not just because they are amazing players, but because they are amazing professionals and people, too. As a manager, all you can ask for is commitment and hard work, and my players show that all the time.

Today we face Wolves. I want to extend a warm welcome to Bruno Lage, his staff and players and the Wolves fans who have arrived here. It should be a great game and a really nice occasion. They are a top team – the Premier League table tells you everything you need to know about their quality.

The work Bruno is doing on the training pitch is clear to see because his side are playing really well. I am really looking forward to seeing how my players can deal with their qualities.

Thank for your support, guys. It means so much and it makes us better. Enjoy the game!

Manchester City 1, Wolves 0

Goal: Sterling (66)

Line-up: Ederson, Cancelo, Dias, Laporte, Zinchenko, Rodrigo, Gundogan (Foden 56), Bernardo Silva, Grealish (De Bruyne 73), Sterling, Jesus.
Subs not used: Steffen, Walker, Stones, Ake, Fernandinho, Mahrez, Palmer.

Raheem Sterling scored the only goal of the game – his 100th in the Premier League – as City beat a well-organised Wolves side to extend our lead at the top of the table.

The England forward struck from the spot after Max Kilamn was adjuged to have blocked Bernardo Silva's cross with his arm.

It was a day of significant milestones at the Etihad, with Ederson's 100th clean sheet for City adding to Sterling's 100th Premier League goal.

Pep's post-match reaction: 'Players are always important, but they sometimes drop. They have highs and lows. I am unfair sometimes, they play well and I don't play them, I don't have an excuse. Raheem scored goals lately and is so committed and aggressive he has been incredibly important over the years. But players have to perform every single game. He is really good, aggressive, and attacks, and this is important. Eddie, I remember at Aston Villa saved some big saves, the big keepers don't have many saves to do but when they have to do it, they do it. When you are 1-0 (up) we started to lose simple balls that were not necessary. But we did and we lost a ball and the counter-attack. We didn't defend the high positions, we dropped too much. We conceded actions. It's good because we will improve for the future. With ten players from Wolves, it's so difficult to play against a team like this. The spaces are so minor. They are so good at defending. In the last 10 games, they lost just two. Last week late in the game against Liverpool. We knew how difficult it would be and we had to be patient. In general we were good. We were not so clever in the final third, some players dropped their performance and some players are coming into their best. We conceded one chance in 94 minutes.

> ### Post-match notes
>
> Raheem Sterling became only the 32nd player to enter the Premier League 100 club with his opener in this game. And at 27 years and three days, he is the eighth youngest player to reach the milestone. This was Ederson's 100th shutout in City colours — in just 212 games.

On City centurions Raheem Sterling and Ederson...

It's a great number at Raheem's age, 100 goals is a lot, congratulations. Like the 100 clean sheets from Eddie, but congratulations to both and to the team, of course.

Raheem scored goals lately and is so committed and aggressive he has been incredibly important over the years.

Eddie, I remember at Aston Villa saved some big saves, the big keepers don't have many saves to do but when they have to do it, they do it.

v Leeds
Tuesday, December 14

'IF WE WANT TO BE SUCCESSFUL THIS SEASON, THEN WE WILL NEED TO FIGHT FOR EVERY BALL AND EVERY POINT'

Premier League

HELLO everyone and welcome back to the Etihad Stadium for this evening's game against Leeds.

We will need our fans tonight. Leeds are one of the best teams in the Premier League. They play with intensity and have quality in all areas. And in Marcelo Bielsa, they have a special manager who organises his team brilliantly. I am under no illusions; this game will be one of the toughest we will play this season.

I love to watch Leeds play football. They are fast, aggressive and always look to win games. I am excited to play them – it's always a great test whenever you play against one of Bielsa's teams.

It will be a completely different task to Saturday's game against Wolves. They defended really well. When teams come here and sit back and then wait for the right moment to counter attack, you cannot make mistakes – and on Saturday, we did not make any mistakes, which is really good.

We restricted them to very few shots – they did not have one with 11 players on the pitch – so we did so many aspects of the game really, really well.

In many ways, this game was good for us because we will learn and improve for the future.

With ten players, it's always so difficult to play against a team like this. The spaces are so minor. They are so good at defending.

In the 10 games before Saturday, they lost just two.

And in the game against Liverpool, they made it so tough. We knew how difficult it would be and we had to be patient.

In general, we were good. We were not so clever in the final third, but we managed to get the win and it was a very important three points.

I am expecting this to be the most difficult Premier League season I have faced. Every year I get the feeling the Premier League gets harder because all the teams get better. From what I have seen so far, that is the case. If we want to be successful, we need to fight for every ball and every point.

But the great thing for me is I have a squad of players who are so determined and incredibly committed. They make me proud every single day and I know I can trust them to give everything for Manchester City.

Enjoy the game – it should be a fantastic evening. And as always, thank you for your support.

Manchester City 7, Leeds 0

Goals: Foden (8), Grealish (13), De Bruyne (32, 62), Mahrez (49), Stones (74), Ake (78)

Line-up: Ederson, Stones, Dias (Ake 65), Laporte, Zinchenko, Rodrigo (Fernandinho 56), De Bruyne, Bernardo (Gundogan 46), Mahrez, Foden, Grealish.
Subs not used: Steffen, Sterling, Jesus, Egan-Riley, Palmer, Wilson-Esbrand.

Pep Guardiola became the quickest manager to reach 500 Premier League goals as Manchester City thrashed Leeds United 7-0 to go four points clear at the top of the table.

The defending champions outclassed the visitors to secure our sixth consecutive league victory with a performance which is up there with the best we have produced this season.

Phil Foden volleyed in the opener from the edge of the area to bring up Guardiola's latest milestone and our lead was doubled five minutes later when the impressive Jack Grealish rose highest to power a header past Illan Mesliery, before Kevin De Bruyne whipped a low drive across Meslier to ensure we went in three goals to the good at half-time.

City continued in a similar vein after the break, with Mahrez adding a fourth and De Bruyne firing into the roof of the net from 25-yards for the fifth.

John Stones made it 6-0 when he lashed home from close range before Nathan Ake completed a fantastic display when he headed home from Foden's corner to secure our 33rd win of 2021, which sees City equal Liverpool's English football record for the most victories in a calendar year which they set in 1982.

Pep's post-match reaction: 'We played a really good game. We dropped five points against Leeds last season with the same guys we had today, except Jack. It was a good game. The vibe at the stadium was phenomenal. It was sold out today and when this happens the players feel it. Thanks so much to the fans. It was a pleasure. We dropped five points last season (against Leeds). Comfortable is nothing. We did a good job. I saw the game against Chelsea and they deserved a point. I know how good they are. Doing what they do is unique. They are the best at it. But the tempo and the patience that we played with was good to win the game.'

Post-match notes

Pep Guardiola reached 500 Premier League goals in just his 207th game, which is quicker than any other manager in the competition. Jurgen Klopp was the previous record holder having done so in 234 games. Meanwhile, Riyad Mahrez is the first player in Premier League history to score on his 100th appearance for two different sides in the competition, doing so with City and Leicester.

Sunday, December 19
Premier League
Newcastle United 0, Manchester City 4

Goals: Dias (5), Cancelo (27), Mahrez (64), Sterling (86)

Line-up: Ederson, Cancelo, Zinchenko, Dias (Stones 70),
Laporte, Rodrigo (Fernandinho 68), De Bruyne, Bernardo,
Mahrez (Palmer 77), Jesus, Sterling.
Subs not used: Steffen, Ake, Gundogan, Grealish,
Foden, Wilson-Esbrand.

City secured the Christmas No.1 spot with another comprehensive victory, this time away to Newcastle.

Two goals in each half secured a 4-0 victory that ensured the champions are top of the festive Premier League chart, with an eighth successive win also setting a new record for victories (34) in a calendar year.

Ruben Dias, Joao Cancelo, Riyad Mahrez and Raheem Sterling were all on target in a game where the home side gave as good as they got in an energetic and committed display.

Pep's post-match reaction: 'It was a good result, exceptional in a not very good performance at all, we were lucky for the goal we scored at the beginning of the game. The second goal, the action from Joao was brilliant, it belongs to him but the way we played in the first half was one of the poorest of the season. The first half was a dangerous position. The second half was much, much better. During the season this can happen. It's normal. You can't be brilliant all the time. We more than deserved the victory but we know we can do better and better. In these types of games you might not be so brilliant, or consistent like we were for the simple things we missed, not the complicated ones. (But) to take a result is so important in this long season ahead of us.'

Post-match notes

This was City's 34th league victory of 2021 — a new Premier League record. City had now also scored 106 goals in 2021 — the most in a calendar year since the Premier League began in 1992.

On City's willingness to evolve being key to their success...

People won't be here for ten years all the time. Players move, it happens often, and the Club has to be prepared for that.

Clubs can't stop, they must follow and take the right decision. Sometimes it works, sometimes it doesn't.

The Club has to be ready to find a solution but it's normal. It happens all the time and it will happen in the future, it's not a big problem.

Pep Guardiola

v Leicester City
Sunday, December 26

'TO SET TWO NEW RECORDS IS SPECIAL AND SAYS EVERYTHING ABOUT THE CONSISTENCY OF MY PLAYERS'

Premier League

HELLO everyone and welcome to the Etihad Stadium. Firstly, I want to wish City fans everywhere a very Happy Christmas! I hope everybody was able to enjoy yesterday with their family and friends. I know it is such a difficult time for the whole of society and it's more important than ever to spend time with our loved ones.

We gained another very important win at Newcastle last Sunday but, although we more than deserved the victory, we know we can do better and better.

We have to build again to avoid a performance like the first half and to do it better but to get the result is so important. It's still a long season for us to try and go on to win the Premier League. There are many games to play and many things can happen. For us, it's important just to stay focused.

However, to beat Newcastle and set two new English football records was really special. We have won more league games – and more away games – than any team in the history of football in this country.

These records prove what I always say about my players. They are so consistent. The only way you can win that many games in a year is by being professional and always working hard, and that is exactly what they do, every single day. It is such a pleasure to manage them.

Today we face Leicester City, a team with so much quality.

Finally, I want to take this opportunity to thank our supporters for all the support you have provided us in 2021. It's been a really challenging year, but you have been constant in your support of the team.

I want to wish all of you the very best for the New Year. Enjoy the game!

Manchester City 6, Leicester City 3

Goals: De Bruyne (5), Mahrez (14), Gundogan (21),
Sterling (25, 87), Laporte (69)

Line-up: Ederson, Cancelo, Dias, Laporte, Zinchenko, Fernandinho,
Gundogan, Bernardo, Mahrez, Sterling, De Bruyne (Foden 71).
Subs not used: Steffen, Carson, Ake, Jesus, Grealish,
Kayky, Mbete, Palmer.

Manchester City made it nine Premier League wins in succession to move six points clear at the top of the table after a remarkable 6-3 victory over Leicester in our final home fixture of 2021.

In an extraordinary game at the Etihad that will live long in the memory, City were 4-0 up inside 25 minutes thanks to goals from Kevin De Bruyne, Ilkay Gundogan, Riyad Mahrez and Raheem Sterling, before Leicester hit three goals in the space of ten second-half minutes to turn the contest on its head.

But Aymeric Laporte's emphatic header made it 5-3, before Sterling scored his second late on to seal the victory.

It was chaotic, breathless and thoroughly entertaining – the highest-scoring Boxing Day fixture in the Premier League era.

Pep's post-match reaction: '(Today was) A roller coaster. It was a typical Boxing Day game, (with) lots of goals. It was entertaining for everyone. Another victory, so important to continue our run. Now we rest for three days and go to the next game. No (I didn't expect such a second half comeback). But even in the first half, we spoke about this at half-time, it was 4-0 and we were creating – but every time they had the ball they arrived in the final third and created chances. The game was open. They are a big team with a lot of quality. Then they changed to 5-4-1. We know the quality in the build-up – Vestergaard is a very good player., Kelechi, Lookman… In the last six games in the Premier League against them we won five, but it is always really tough. When you play teams like Leicester, always you suffer. They have quality in these positions. We struggled a little when we lost the ball. At 4-2 the mindset of the players changed, and at 4-3 we are closer to losing and we have doubts. But we were patient, we had chances and won the game. Football is unpredictable, everything can happen, and they scored two goals. But it was not because we had to solve much. I give credit to them. Sometimes the teams are good and when that happens, they can do what they did. The game was really good. We could have scored much more.'

Wednesday, December 29
Premier League
Brentford 0, Manchester City 1

Goal: Foden (16)

Line-up: Ederson, Cancelo, Dias, Laporte, Ake, Fernandinho,
De Bruyne, Bernardo, Foden, Jesus, Grealish.
Subs not used: Steffen, Carson, Sterling, Gundogan, Zinchenko,
Mahrez, Mbete, Palmer.

Manchester City signed off 2021 with a slender but deserved victory over Brentford to move eight points clear at the top of the Premier League.

Phil Foden scored the only goal of the game as City capitalised on Chelsea's draw at Brighton on the same evening and Liverpool's defeat to Leicester the night before to extend our advantage at the summit heading into the new year.

On his return to the starting XI, Foden scored a classy volley from Kevin De Bruyne's superb 16th minute cross to clinch Pep Guardiola's side's 10th consecutive win in the league.

Pep's post-match reaction: 'This was the best performance we could play. It was so intelligent because they are the best team in the Premier League on set-pieces (as they showed) with the chance they had on the first corner. The second half was much, much better. We played the game in this stadium, against this team how it must be played. The quality of the players made the difference. It's a good victory. Now we recover as much as possible because at 12.30 on 1 January we have another game. We won a game, but we are at the end of December with many games to play. We are eight points in front, but with 54 still to play. The team after all the years together still fight. Today we needed this type of rhythm. If you make attack quick, they will attack quicker with Toney… Every time they put the ball in the box they are so good. Just look at the results Brentford have done this season. It has been so tight. They are exceptional at what they do and that's why the game we played was perfect today. There are 54 points to play for. Chelsea and Liverpool are more than exceptional. One is the champion of Europe and Liverpool have been our big rival in recent years. 54 points still to play and every game we are just thinking the next game we have.'

Post-match notes

This is the fourth time we've had a run of 10 or more consecutive league wins under Pep Guardiola. No other manager in Premier League history has had more than two separate runs of 10 or more wins. It meant City ended 2021 having record 36 victories and 19 away wins in the league, both of which are English top-flight records.

On what makes Fernandinho such a great captain...

He is an incredible captain that we have because he didn't play much this season because Rodri has been exceptional. He always tries to help the team, the guys who don't play, myself, the staff. He is so generous. He is just thinking about what the team need and what is best for the team.

This is a real captain, when they always think about what is best for the team and the club. That is why he is so generous when he doesn't play and when he plays, he always plays good.

We will need him because we have many games and Rodri cannot play all season, it is impossible.

That is why against Brentford and Leicester, he was exceptional.

JAN

2022

With Kevin De Bruyne pulling the strings, we returned to the Wembley trail with a convincing win over Swindon and extended our lead at the top of the Premier League, with Pep recording his 500th point as City boss in the process

1st: Arsenal (PL) A
7th: Swindon Town (FAC) A
15th: Chelsea (PL) H
22nd: Southampton (PL) A

**Saturday, January 1
Premier League
Arsenal 1, Manchester City 2**

Goals: Mahrez (57), Rodrigo (93)

*Line-up: Ederson, Cancelo, Dias, Laporte, Ake, Rodrigo, De Bruyne,
Bernardo, Mahrez, Sterling, Jesus (Gundogan 63).
Subs not used: Steffen, Walker, Grealish, Fernandinho, Kayky, Mbete,
Palmer, McAtee.*

A stoppage-time goal from Rodrigo ensured Manchester City beat 10-man Arsenal in a lively encounter to go 11 points clear at the top of the Premier League.

The Spaniard prodded home a loose ball from close range in the 93rd minute to complete a second half fightback and secure our 11th consecutive victory in the competition.

Pep Guardiola's side fell behind when Bukayo Saka swept home Kieran Tierney's pass to finish off a slick passing move during a first half in which the Gunners were in the ascendancy.

However, the game was turned upside down when Riyad Mahrez converted a 57th minute penalty to level things up.

It was an absorbing encounter in North London that looked destined to end all square until Laporte's blocked volley fell kindly into the path of Rodrigo, who made no mistake from 10-yards.

Pep's post-match reaction: '(Winning) 11 games in a row is so great in this period. Just take a look at our bench today, it was four guys from the Academy. We had many cases from COVID this season and injuries. Phil Foden, Kyle today and Rodri the first day since COVID time. This period today we were incredibly tired, mentally and physically. Arsenal were better today, but football happens in these situations, sometimes it comes on our side. Congratulations (to my players). We are not a team to (normally) score goals in extra time. I don't remember the last time we scored a goal after 90 minutes! Maybe two or three years ago when Raheem put the ball in the net against Southampton. We're not a team with this characteristic but of course with 10 v 11 they changed with five at the back and tried to win the game. Arsenal were better, we faced a team in the last years who struggled to be in the top four and started the season at the bottom, but they are in the top four now and had six or seven days from last game. We had two and a half, we came back and didn't have energy. That's why we tried to put one more in the middle to have control and more passes. Football, we try to analyse many things, but it can be like a coin. Sometimes it's on your side, sometimes it's not. That's the reality, but at the same time we know how much it means to win here at the Emirates against Arsenal, the moment they're in. We knew it was difficult and now we have time to rest.'

Friday, January 7
FA Cup
Swindon 1, Manchester City 4

Goals: Silva (14), Jesus (28), Gundogan (59), Palmer (82)

*Line-up: Steffen, Walker, Cancelo, Ake (Mbete 86), Dias,
Rodrigo, Gundogan (Lavia 83), De Bruyne (McAtee 66),
Bernardo, Palmer (Kayky 86), Jesus.
Subs not used: Carson, Slicker, Laporte, Bobb, Egan-Riley.*

City are back on the Wembley trail after a thoroughly
professional performance against Swindon Town.

First-half goals from Bernardo and Gabriel Jesus gave
the Blues a 2-0 lead at the break.

Ilkay Gundogan added a third just before the
hour-mark with Jesus missing a penalty a couple of
minutes later.

The home side pulled a consolation goal back through
Harry McKirdy on 79 minutes, before the impressive
Cole Palmer responded with a stunning effort on 82 to
complete a 4-1 victory.

*Rodolfo Borrell's reaction: 'We were facing a big challenge in the
FA Cup. It is always challenging – if you take it seriously and
don't start on the front foot, you are in trouble and it can be the
difference in terms of quality. I think we started very well on the*

front foot and very quickly we scored a goal, then another and could have had two or three more which is the reality. Towards the end of the first half we maybe allowed too many counter-attacks and it was going back and forth and in the second half there were some counter-attacks again, but the game was already decided by this stage. But in terms of fielding a strong team, we take this competition very seriously and we are very much aware of the history of the FA Cup in this country and what it means. We have achieved three Premier League titles and many others, but our FA Cup win was one of our proudest.'

On City's superb defensive record...

We defend with the ball. We believe you don't need lots of players in the box to defend well.

When the opponent has the ball far away from the goal and when you have the ball, that's the best way to defend.

To concede a goal, the opponent has to have the ball and the less they have it, the more chances we have to have a clean sheet and be solid. And after we can talk about what we have to do with the ball.

But if you look at the best teams in the Premier League right now it is because most of them are offensive and have the ball a high per cent.

I am very pleased for that (defensive record). Be offensive but, at the same time, be solid and concede few goals.

Pep Guardiola

v Chelsea
Saturday, January 15
—

'TO WIN OUR
LAST 11 PREMIER
LEAGUE GAMES
IS AN AMAZING
ACHIEVEMENT AND
I AM SO PROUD OF
MY PLAYERS'

Premier League

HELLO everyone and welcome back to the Etihad Stadium. It's been a while since we played in Manchester!

Since our last game here on Boxing Day, we've played three really tough matches away from home, so it's a pleasure to be back here today with our fans behind us.

Your support means so much to us and if we are successful again this season, you will be a vital part of that.

I want to take the time to thank everyone who travelled with us over the New Year period. We know it isn't an easy time for fans, but the noise you guys made at Brentford, Arsenal and Swindon was perfect. The players always say what a difference it makes, so a massive thank you to all of you.

We've had a fantastic run of results and I am so proud of my players. We've won our last 11 Premier League games, which is an amazing achievement given how strong this league is and how many games we have played in a short space of time.

We've also moved through to the Fourth Round of the FA Cup, too, which is a competition we really want to win. So, all in all, I am delighted with the way we are playing right now.

To show that level of consistency given the challenges we face with Covid is extraordinary and makes me so proud to be the manager of this squad. Of course, our consistency stretched right across 2021 and I am so proud of what we achieved last year. Hopefully you guys enjoyed watching us and I really hope we can continue like this in 2022.

Today we face Chelsea, a team who have top players in every position. They have improved a lot and they are now a challenger for the Premier League title this season.

I want to welcome Thomas, his staff and players here today. He is a top manager and one who I love to play against. He has a clear way of playing and always has clever ideas. It's such a challenge trying to beat him but that is my job today.

This is a very important game for us, and we know how hard it will be. My staff have analysed Chelsea, like we do for every game, and the players are ready. All I hope is we play our football in our own style and show personality. If we do that, we have a chance of getting a good result. It should be a great game and a fantastic occasion.

Thank you for being here today and hopefully you we can continue our great start to the new year.

Manchester City 1, Chelsea 0

Goal: De Bruyne (70)

*Line-up: Ederson, Walker, Stones, Laporte, Cancelo,
Rodrigo, De Bruyne (Gundogan 84), Bernardo,
Foden (Jesus 88), Grealish, Sterling.
Subs not used: Steffen, Dias, Fernandinho, Mbete,
McAtee, Lavia, Wilson-Esbrand.*

A moment of magic from Kevin De Bruyne gave Manchester City victory over Chelsea and strengthened our position at the top of the Premier League.

The Belgian curled a stunning effort into the bottom corner from 25-yards in the 70th minute to send City 13 points clear of the second-placed Blues as we recorded our 12th consecutive win in the competition.

It sealed a deserved victory for Pep Guardiola's men, who controlled a tight contest throughout and might have won by more but for a brilliant save from Kepa, who denied Jack Grealish with his thigh in the first half.

Pep's post-match reaction: 'Absolutely [it's a big victory]. They are the European champions. They deserved it. I know how difficult they are; how well they defend. They are a team that sits back and tries to beat you in transition and we beat them in one transition. We were fantastic. We defended incredibly well. All players gave everything. It is an important victory because we are playing against a big contender. Now, we rest and then it is Southampton. In January, no-one is the champion. We can think about Chelsea, but Liverpool have one game in hand. If they win (the game in hand) versus Leeds, it's eight points and eight points in January is nothing. We spoke before the game. I want to win the game if we deserve it and we deserved it. I like football to be fair. I was happy to win against Arsenal, but we didn't deserve it. When you deserve it, it feels better. All the big contenders, we beat away. Many tough games are away and now all of them come to our home. Against Leicester we did well in the first half especially and today as well and we just have to continue. We played really well against teams in the middle of the table. To win 12 in a row you sometimes need luck – the Arsenal game – but the other games we were better. Leicester, Brighton, in every game we were good. I don't know what is going to happen. I don't care. What I care about is that after everything we have won after six years, these guys still give everything for this club. That is difficult to find. We are humble to run without the ball every game. This is our biggest achievement. To win and win, in this country, in this league, this is my best title I have and the best I will have when I leave.'

Post-match notes

Kevin De Bruyne has now scored five goals against Chelsea in the Premier League; the most by any former Chelsea player, who has represented them in the competition. The 30-year-old has scored 21 Premier League goals from outside the box, which is more than other player since his first season at City (2015-16). It is the joint-most in City's history, alongside Sergio Aguero.

On how City – and Liverpool – have raised the standard needed to be Premier League champions...

What Liverpool and Manchester City has done in last three or four years has never before been seen before in this country, never ever.

Now it's more than 90 points [needed] to be champions, before it was 78, 80, 82, 86, 87. I think Antonio Conte with Chelsea started it a little bit when they won the league in my first season here but after, Liverpool and City made a step [forward].

And I think they did well the other opponents – Chelsea, United, Tottenham – but Liverpool and City were out of this world.

And I'm proud after six seasons together or five years of success, in January we are still there in every single game competing.

I repeat many times, what happened after being Champion, the next season of the last 10 champions, they drop, but drop massively and we are there, and that's incredible credit.

Credit to these exceptional players but my job is to put my words behind them and tell them the truth, that's why we have to continue to do it.

Saturday, January 22
Premier League
Southampton 1, Manchester City 1

Goals: Laporte (65)

Line-up: Ederson, Walker, Dias, Laporte, Cancelo, Rodrigo, De Bruyne,
Bernardo, Foden, Grealish, Sterling (Jesus 59).
Subs not used: Carson, Slicker, Stones, Ake, Fernandinho, Gundogan,
McAtee, Wilson-Esbrand.

Aymeric Laporte's second half header earned City a share of the spoils at Southampton in what was a pulsating Premier League encounter at the St Mary's Stadium.

The hosts had taken an early lead through Kyle Walker-Peters' seventh minute shot.

Pep Guardiola's side responded in kind with Laporte deservedly heading home from Kevin De Bruyne's pinpoint free-kick midway through the second half.

City came close to forcing a winner but had to settle for a point as our 12 match Premier League winning run was finally checked.

It was still a landmark occasion though with the draw seeing Guardiola record his 500th point as City boss – achieving the feat in the quickest time in league history.

Pep's post-match reaction: 'I don't need a good result even today winning the game (to know) the title race will not be over. In January no-one is champions. There are many games, many tough games like today and that's all. Today we played to play good and tried to defend our badge and our people as best as possible and the title will always be a consequence of what we have done. Today was really good. We played really well – maybe for 10 or 15 minutes we were not aggressive enough, but the last 20 minutes was excellent and the second half was excellent, too. We made an excellent performance for 90 minutes against a top side. It is always so tough to play against them as they have experience in many, many things but we made an exceptional performance. Unfortunately, in the first half we conceded a goal, but I think this was one of our best performances of the season, by far. They were incredibly organised and this is one of the best performances we played against them. Yes, the result was not good, but in terms of performance and the way we played, it was excellent. We played better than in the Arsenal game, when we won, and today we drew. Sometimes you deserve it and you don't win, but the way we played here was excellent.'

Post-match notes

This was Kevin De Bruyne's 80th Premier League assist, taking him level with David Beckham and ninth in the all-time league list. De Bruyne, however, achieved that landmark in 68 fewer appearances.

FEB

2022

With Raheem Sterling embarking on
a rich vein of goalscoring form and the
team hitting some important landmarks
both at home and abroad, the only blot on
February's landscape came at the hands
of some familiar foes as Spurs ended our
15-match unbeaten run in a
smash-and-grab at the Etihad

5th: Fulham (FAC) H
9th: Brentford (PL) A
12th: Norwich (PL) A
15th: Sporting CP (CL) A
19th: Tottenham Hotspur (PL) H
26th: Everton (PL) A

**v Fulham
Saturday, February 5**

'WINNING THE FA CUP IN 2019 WAS SUCH A PROUD MOMENT AND ONE WE ALL WANT TO EXPERIENCE AGAIN'

FA Cup fourth round

HELLO City fans and welcome back to the Etihad. It's a pleasure to be back here after a long time away and I can't wait for this game today. Always, playing in front of our fans is something we love, and your support is so important to us.

Welcome, of course, to everyone from Fulham and the supporters who have travelled here today. Everyone can see how well they are playing – the Championship table says everything you need to know. They are in the habit of winning, which makes them very, very dangerous opponents.

Marco Silva is an outstanding manager. His teams have a really clear way of playing and his players always know exactly what he expects of them. Fulham's performances this season – the quality of their football and the goals they have scored – tells you what a fantastic coach he is. I have been so impressed with them and I am sure we will see them again in the Premier League next season.

The FA Cup is the oldest and most beautiful domestic cup competition in the world. There have been so many amazing FA Cup stories written over the years, and to be a manager here in England and have the chance to compete in this competition is an honour and privilege.

When we won the FA Cup in 2019, it was one of our proudest moments since coming here to City. It was such a special day for me, my staff, my players, our fans and the whole club. I will never, ever forget it and I know everyone wants to experience that again. We will do everything we can, starting today, to try and bring the trophy back here to Manchester.

Last week's break was fantastic for myself, my staff and all the players. After such a challenging period, it was great for us to be able to relax our bodies and minds, spend time with our families and recover ahead of the rest of the season. It is so important to take those opportunities because the demands on players is huge.

There's still a long way to go this season but, so far, I am delighted with my players and our consistent level of performance. Hopefully we can continue in this way.

Thank you for your support and enjoy today's game.

Manchester City 4, Fulham 1

Goals: Gundogan (6), Stones (13), Mahrez (53, 57)

Line-up: Steffen, Walker, Cancelo (Zinchenko 67), Stones, Ake, Fernandinho, Grealish (Delap 77), Gundogan, De Bruyne (Sterling 68), Mahrez (McAtee 78), Foden (Bernardo 78). Subs not used: Ederson, Dias, Laporte, Rodrigo.

City came from behind to see off a lively Fulham outfit 4-1 in the FA Cup fourth round.

The Championship leaders raced into an early lead through Fabio Carvalho before Ilkay Gundogan and John Stones responded with two quick goals, before a Riyad Mahrez double after the break ended Fulham's hopes of an upset.

Pep's post-match reaction: 'I am going to tell you something, I know exactly which team we faced today and which team we beat. When a team is top of the Championship, it is because they are good. Top side, Marco has created an incredible team. We spoke a lot with the players about how difficult it would be and we should fight and run and defend well. They are a team who monopolise the ball. The first half the pressing was not good, that was my fault because we expected one movement that didn't work well. The second half was much better and of course the quality of our players made the difference. We started really well (against Fulham), had one or two chances and the first chance they got they scored a goal. (But) Phil (Foden) immediately got the ball and made a diagonal and we scored a goal. This is what I like, because the toughest moments are coming, and it is how you react. How you react in the bad moments, that's what the big teams do. That is what I want to see in my team. For me, what's more important than winning 5-0 is how we react to the bad moments in 90 minutes. We try to play and train at a maximum level at 100%, but sometimes it doesn't happen. Even if you win a lot of games it doesn't happen. Maybe against adversity you don't get what you deserve. That's not a problem and the next game is the same but one day, when you fight against adversity, you will get what you deserve. I want to win always, of course, but I want to win when we deserve it. For that, you have to do it better and better and in the bad moments be resilient. We are very pleased to be in the next round. This round showed us there can be many surprises and we won against a very top team.'

v Brentford
Wednesday, February 9

'BRENTFORD ARE AGGRESIVE AND MAKE IT SO, SO HARD, BUT HAVING OUR FANS HERE WITH US WILL HELP'

Premier League

GOOD evening, everyone and welcome back to the Etihad Stadium.

It was so good to see the team play so well on against Fulham on Saturday after a week of rest. My players looked fresh and absolutely determined to win. The FA Cup is a special competition, full of difficulties and complications. The way we played, particularly in the second half, showed everyone what our intentions are. We want to bring the trophy back to Manchester.

But believe me, that was one of the toughest matches we have faced this season. Marco Silva has done an incredible job there. If you are top of the Championship, it's because you are a top side and they showed that here on Saturday. They attack so well, score so many goals and they gave us so many difficult moments. Congratulations to them for the way they played, and I feel sure they will be back in the Premier League next season.

It was a really amazing weekend of football. The FA Cup is full of surprises – so many teams from lower divisions are dangerous. If we are going to win it, we will have to fight in every single round.

We go to Peterborough next, which I am really looking forward to. We will make sure we watch them closely and we will be ready. It will be a very different challenge to what we have faced before and our preparation will be vital.

Today Brentford are here, and I want to welcome

everyone who has travelled with them today – their staff, players, fans and directors. We know from our game against them in London in December what to expect today – it won't be easy.

They are aggressive, they fight for every ball, have energy and pace and they make it so, so hard. Even in their recent matches when maybe results have not been good, the effort and attitude of Thomas' players is always spot on. I expect a very difficult night but having our fans with us will help. I hope we can entertain you guys again because when you enjoy what you see, it makes it so much more enjoyable for the players, too.

Thank you, as always, for your support. It means so much. You were perfect on Saturday, and I am delighted we could make it through so we can continue in the FA Cup. You deserve it.

This is a crucial period in our season, and we will need you in the coming months.

Enjoy the game and thank for being with us.

Manchester City 2, Brentford 0

Goals: Mahrez (40), De Bruyne (69)

Line-up: Ederson, Stones, Dias, Laporte, Cancelo, Rodrigo, De Bruyne, Bernardo, Sterling, Foden (Gundogan 70), Mahrez (Grealish 65). Subs: Steffen, Walker, Ake, Zinchenko, Fernandinho, Delap, McAtee.

Goals from Riyad Mahrez and Kevin De Bruyne saw City overcome a dogged Brentford at the Etihad and so extend our lead at the top of the Premier League.

Mahrez struck with a 39th minute penalty to score for the seventh successive game after Raheem Sterling had been brought down to send Pep Guardiola's side in at the break holding the advantage.

And De Bruyne then sealed the deal with fine 69th minute effort from another Bees error to secure our 19th league win of the season and move us 12 points clear at the top of the table.

Pep's post-match reaction: 'This was an important victory, three more points to reach 60 with 14 games left, next up Norwich. Riyad Mahrez was especially good and so solid in the penalty, which we struggled with in previous seasons. It was difficult for the wingers as they did not have space, but we won. Joao Cancelo was the best winger we had, he was better than our [traditional] wingers. He was really good, him and John Stones were so important today to create more space for the other guys with their movement.'

Saturday, February 12
Premier League
Norwich 0, Manchester City 4

Goals: Sterling (31, 70, 90), Foden (48)

Line-up: Ederson, Walker, Dias, Ake, Zinchenko,
Fernandinho, Gundogan, Bernardo (McAtee 75),
Mahrez (Kayky 84), Sterling, Foden (Delap 82).
Subs not used: Carson, Stones, Laporte, Rodrigo, De Bruyne, Cancelo.

City made it 14 wins from 15 Premier League matches with a 4-0 victory over a well-organised Norwich side at Carrow Road.

A hat-trick from Raheem Sterling and Phil Foden strike sealed the win and extended our lead at the top of the Premier League to 12 points.

There was a notable milestone for Pep Guardiola, who celebrated the 550th win of his management career – the perfect boost ahead of Tuesday's UEFA Champions League last-16 game against Sporting.

Pep's post-match reaction: 'In general this was a good
performance. We arrived here at the best moment for Norwich
in terms of their results and confidence. We play all these years
seriously and today they proved it again. When Aleks doesn't

play because Joao is in top form, they accept it. They don't have to convince me or their teammates of their quality, they have to perform well. We have a lot of competitions and everyone must be involved. We played three days before and will play again in three days — we need fresh legs. These guys proved they can play in any game. I am sure it will be a massive confidence boost for Raheem. I have known him for six seasons. I know him perfectly well. This season he was outstanding in goals and assists and his contribution to the team. During that period there are highs and lows. It's part of life. Teams are not honeymoons. There are problems and we have to solve them. Nobody doubts how important he is. He is showing that. What I want is for all the players to play good. If we count the amount games he played since we are together, it is a lot. He was a key player.'

Post-match notes

Raheem Sterling had now been involved in 10 goals in his last eight Premier League games against Norwich (eight goals, two assists).

Tuesday, February 15
UEFA Champions League
Sporting CP 0, Manchester City 5

Goals: Mahrez (7), Silva (17, 44), Foden (32), Sterling (58)

Line-up: Ederson, Stones (Zinchenko 61), Dias, Laporte (Ake 85), Cancelo, Rodrigo (Fernandinho 73), De Bruyne, Bernardo (Delap 85), Mahrez, Foden (Gundogan 61), Sterling.
Subs not used: Carson, Slicker, Kayky, Mbete, McAtee, Lavia.

Manchester City seized control of our Champions League last 16 tie with a ruthless display in the first leg against Sporting in Lisbon.

Bernardo Silva scored twice, with Riyad Mahrez and Phil Foden netting one apiece in a rampant first half performance, before Raheem Sterling added a fifth as we became the first team in the competition's history to win five consecutive away games in the knockout stages.

Pep's post-match reaction: 'Don't misunderstand me. I am more than delighted. I know how difficult this competition is. 5-0 is fantastic, today we were so clinical, arrive goal, arrive goal, arrive goal and when that happens it is difficult for the opponent. But we didn't do our build up well. We defended well and we got an incredible result. But we have a duty as a manager and as a team to analyse exactly how we performed individually and collectively. Not just the result. The result is a dream but we can perform better. Not just in the Champions League, but in the Premier League we always concede few. We concede so few shots on target in every game. This is important. We have to take care of the few chances they had. But I say the same, we are not a team that defend well. If you analyse individually we are not defenders, we are an offensive team in most departments. We have to do it with the ball. We have to take better care of it than we did today. Today it was because we were so clinical. We arrived and scored and when that happens it is mentally difficult for the opponent, you get confidence and you relax. Sometimes football is margins. Sometimes you win games for this and all the analysis is how good one team is, how bad the other one is but it is the margin. Maybe you have this duty and you have another one is to see how they perform individually and the team and the plan depends on how they play if we execute it as well or not. Don't misunderstand me, it is a dream, a perfect result and so good for the second leg. But we can do better.'

Post-match notes

City are the first team in Champions League history to lead an away game in the knockout stages by four goals at half-time. And we are the 14th team to score 200 goals in the Champions League, reaching the landmark in 97 games, fewer than any of the other 13 teams to reach that milestone.

February 2022

**v Tottenham Hotspur
Saturday, February 19**

'IT HAS BEEN A REALLY GOOD SEASON SO FAR, BUT IF WE ARE GOING TO WIN TROPHIES WE NEED TO KEEP FIGHTING'

Premier League

HELLO City fans and welcome to the Etihad. It's a pleasure to be back here in Manchester for a game I'm really excited about.

Tottenham are one of the best teams in the Premier League and I always really look forward to playing against them.

They have some amazing players and always in football you want to compete against the best. I am sure this will be a really good game for our fans to enjoy. In almost every game we have played against Tottenham in my time here, it has been a really close, entertaining match and tonight will be the same.

Welcome to Antonio and his staff. He is a winner – he has shown that throughout his career, everywhere he has gone – and I am delighted he is back in the Premier League.

Our trip to Lisbon was really good. Obviously, to win 5-0 away from home in a Champions League last-16 game is fantastic – a dream result for us.

But, honestly, I think we can play much, much better. We lost some easy balls, and we must improve this. Our build up has to be good.

I have made it clear to the players that we must do this better.

We were so clinical – every time we arrived close to their goal in the early stages, we scored. 5-0 didn't really reflect the difference between the sides, but we punished

Sporting with our finishing. When this happens, it is difficult for your opponent.

This was a big step towards the next round, but the players know me, they know what I expect, and they know we can do better. Take care of the ball – that is so, so important.

And what can I say about our fans who travelled to Portugal? Wow! You were incredible! Do not underestimate how much that kind of support helps us. It drives us on and makes us so happy when we can celebrate with you at the end.

It has been a really good season for us so far but there is so much hard work ahead. We want to win trophies, and if we are going to do that we need to keep fighting.

Whatever happens, I am so proud of my players for their efforts. It's honestly such a pleasure working with them every day and seeing their desire to be better. They are relentless and they deserve everything they have achieved so far.

Thank you for your support and enjoy the game.

Manchester City 2, Tottenham 3

Goals: Gundogan (33), Mahrez (90'+2 pen)

Line-up: Ederson, Walker, Cancelo, Dias, Laporte, Rodrigo, Gundogan, De Bruyne, Bernardo, Sterling (Mahrez 67), Foden.
Subs not used: Carson, Stones, Ake, Zinchenko, Fernandinho, Delap, McAtee, Lavia.

City's 15-match unbeaten run was ended in added time by a smash-and-grab Tottenham at the Etihad.

The visitors, playing almost exclusively on the counter-attack, struck early on and though Ilkay Gundogan equalised before half-time, went ahead again after the break through Harry Kane.

But in a frantic finish, a penalty by Riyad Mahrez in the 92nd minute of the game looked to have rescued a point for City, only for Kane to dramatically add another three minutes later – the goal that settled the contest 3-2 in Tottenham's favour.

Pep's post-match reaction: 'We performed well. We were who we normally are. They defended in the 18-yard box. It was so difficult, we had to go outside and after they can run with the quality they had. Every time we played inside, we had to go outside and we crossed and for many actions were not there to score. I think we performed well, honestly. The first goal was the quality they had, the second was difficult to defend. The third was our mistake. It's normal [to lose], especially in the Premier League. The teams at the bottom won all their games [this weekend]. Everyone fights for everything so it will be difficult. We know it. Today happened, we lost a game, we were close to a draw, maybe a win. Congratulations to Tottenham. We will recover this week and onto the next game. We have to fight for every game and every game we will try to win. We have to make a lot of points to be champion and that is what we will try to do. I said a few weeks ago we need to win many games. Every game will be a big, big battle. We knew it, and it will be good to understand how difficult it is. Since October we didn't lose one game in the Premier League. I had the feeling they have fantastic players and a fantastic manager. We knew after three defeats they would be back. There was practically no space in the area. After that, they could keep the ball and with Kane, it gave time to Son who could run. In general we were there all the time. We were there but we couldn't win.'

On how he has changed as a manager…

I know them [the players] much better. I understood as I got older that they want to do well.

Me personally, as a manager, I am not cool enough or clear enough to analyse what happened in the game immediately to the players. There are too many emotions.

Maybe I learned. Sometimes I talked after the game. Sometimes, when I am angry, I say take time, go home and tomorrow we'll talk with the team about what you feel was the real game.

Sometimes you are aggressive, and you are unfair to the players because they want to do well. I have this principle for a long time.

They want to run, they want to fight, they want to win and when it doesn't happen, sometimes it is because it was not clear enough or they have a bad day.

It's happened. They have the responsibility to avoid it. It is the most important part of the week, the 90 minutes, but it has happened.

Pep Guardiola

Saturday, February 26
Premier League
Everton 0, Manchester City 1

Goal: Foden (82)

*Line-up: Ederson, Stones, Dias, Laporte, Cancelo, Rodrigo, Gundogan
(Mahrez 77), De Bruyne, Bernardo, Foden, Sterling (Jesus 77).
Subs not used: Carson, Slicker, Walker, Ake, Grealish,
Zinchenko, Fernandinho.*

Manchester City returned to winning ways in the
Premier League as Phil Foden's late goal broke
Everton's stubborn resistance in a hard-fought contest
at Goodison Park.

Pep Guardiola's men had been frustrated for 81
minutes until Foden nipped in front of Michael
Keane to turn Bernardo Silva's deflected cross past
Jordan Pickford to ensure City bounced back from last
weekend's defeat to Tottenham Hotspur in positive
fashion.

*Pep's post-match reaction: '(Over) 90 minutes we were better.
The second half was much better. It is not easy, Richarlison
(was marking) man to man to Rodrigo, they allowed us to play
for the central defenders, and didn't allow us to play inside.
Always that is difficult. We were patient. In the second half
we conceded some counter attacks but we were much, much*

better and at the end we deserved to win. I have to admit, really important [to get the win]. The second half was much better for the consequences of the first half. We moved them and attacked better. Goodison Park for us is always so difficult. (It was a) good victory, another step. In general, we controlled in the second half, we had chances, not a lot because it was not possible but the second was half much, much better. Our fans when we play away are incredible and amazing. I would love to hug them every single game to thank them because wherever we we go, they are there. We feel their warmth and the players notice. Our fans away from home are extraordinary.'

On what's needed to win the Premier League...

There's no doubt about that – the margin against Liverpool is nothing. We have to win a lot – more than 90 points – 95, 96 to be champions. We can lose, but it's the way we lose [that's important]. You can lose in different ways.

Many times, when we lose, we lose as a great team and we have to continue in this way.

I was born in Barcelona and their academy taught me everything. The best way, even there, is to think everything can go wrong.

The warnings to yourself have to be as an individual player or as a team that tomorrow you can go down and lose and lose and lose. That's the best way to approach games.

We made an incredible run in the Premier League so

far and Liverpool is still there round the corner. That shows how amazing and difficult our opponent is.

We know, of course, we can lose and be bad and drop points – this is not the issue – it's how you behave in those moments when you lose games.

Against Brentford, we were 2-0 up and Kevin De Bruyne, the best player in the Premier League last season, ran 40 metres back to help John Stones at right back.

We can't ask any more than that after winning what we have won individually and collectively.

We have to fight to win the Premier League and if we want to win, we will have to win an incredible amount of points against an incredible opponent we've faced many times.

MAR

2022

After seeing off Sporting CP in the Champions League and Peterborough United in the FA Cup, another unbeaten month in the Premier League meant the treble was very much still on, with the regal Kevin De Bruyne continuing at his masterful best

1st: Peterborough United (FAC) A
6th: Manchester United (PL) H
9th: Sporting CP (CL) H
14th: Crystal Palace (PL) A
20th: Southampton (FAC) A

Tuesday, March 1
FA Cup fifth round
Peterborough 0, Manchester City 2

Goals: Mahrez (60), Grealish (67)

*Line-up: Ederson, Cancelo, Dias (Stones 46), Ake (Laporte 46),
Zinchenko, Fernandinho, Gundogan, Foden, Grealish, Mahrez, Jesus.
Subs not used: Carson, Slicker, Sterling, Rodrigo, De Bruyne, Bernardo.*

Manchester City's bid to win three major trophies
continues unabated thanks to a 2-0 win over
Peterborough in the FA Cup.

In a hard-fought fifth-round tie at London Road, the
Championship side kept City at bay in the first half,
with our play often disjointed and lacking rhythm.

But Riyad Mahrez produced a moment of quality to
fire past Steven Benda and break the deadlock with an
hour gone, before Phil Foden's outrageous long-range
pass set up Jack Grealish to score a second seven
minutes later.

*Pep's post-match reaction: 'We are in the next round and in
the end, the quality of our players made the difference. They
were brilliant goals. The quality of Riyad and the second goal
the same. It was good. We created chances. All of them were
brilliant. Riyad always had this quality in the final third –*

he is the best we have. He scored a fantastic goal. So proud of the game he played. The pass from Phil (for the Grealish goal) was excellent – the control was excellent from Jack. He was aggressive in the final third and is back from injury and played a really good level. It's not an easy period for Oleks. His family, his country but playing football is the best for him at the moment.'

Post-match notes

Before the game started, Fernandinho handed Oleksandr Zinchenko the captain's armband as an act of solidarity after a difficult week for the Ukrainian given the unfolding war in his homeland.

Pep Guardiola

**v Manchester United
Sunday, March 6**

'AS A MANAGER THERE IS NOTHING BETTER THAN TESTING YOURSELF AGAINST THE BEST TEAMS'

Premier League

HELLO City fans and welcome to the Etihad Stadium for this Manchester derby. It should be a fantastic game.

Welcome also to Ralf Rangnick, his staff, players and all the Manchester United supporters. I aways say there is nothing better in football than testing yourself against the best teams.

As a manager, I like to be challenged and Manchester United, with their quality and history, always provide us with a really difficult game that requires us to be at our best.

We know their strengths and where they can hurt us, but we have prepared really well for this match. My players have been amazing all week in training, just like they have all season. I love working with this squad, it's honestly a great pleasure to be their manager.

I was really pleased with the way we played on Tuesday against Peterborough. Except for the first six minutes of second half, the rest was really good, especially when you consider the difficulties with the pitch and how aggressive they are. In the end, we deserved the win and the two goals we scored were excellent.

I am delighted to be there in the FA Cup quarter-finals. It's a competition we all love and when we won it in 2019, it was such a proud moment. I can assure all our fans we are trying to bring that beautiful trophy back here to Manchester.

But Tuesday was not just about the result or our

progress in the FA Cup. Aleks Zinchenko felt the incredible support of all the City fans who again travelled so far to watch us.

And it isn't just our fans who have offered him support. He's had messages from people all across the world throughout the last week as the situation in his home country has continued to escalate. The football community has come together, and I know it has helped him and offered him strength. Everyone wants the violence to end and peace to return.

Before Tuesday's game, Fernandinho gave him the captain's armband, which was a gesture everyone in the dressing room was fully behind. It meant so much to him and I was delighted with how he played in the circumstances.

The whole club is behind him, and he knows we will support him throughout. Whatever he needs, we will be there.

Thank you everyone and enjoy the game.

Manchester City 4, Manchester United 1

Goals: De Bruyne (5, 28), Mahrez (68, 90)

Line-up: Ederson, Walker, Cancelo, Stones, Laporte, Rodrigo, De Bruyne (Gundogan 80), Bernardo, Grealish, Foden, Mahrez. Subs not used: Carson, Sterling, Jesus, Zinchenko, Fernandinho, Delap, Mbete, McAtee.

City produced a stunning display to beat Manchester United 4-1 and restore a six-point advantage over Liverpool at the top of the Premier League.

Two Kevin De Bruyne strikes ensured City edged a keenly-contested first 45 minutes, going in 2-1 up – but the champions shifted through the gears in the second-half.

Riyad Mahrez added two more to his tally in the second period, with Pep Guardiola's men utterly dominant and perhaps a little disappointed not to have won by an even bigger margin.

Pep's post-match reaction: 'The display was excellent. We let them run a lot in the first half but we made an excellent performance. I am the biggest critic of my team, but today in the second half we played really good. We struggled to make a better build up [in the first half] but I don't think they created much problems. We felt from the first minute of the second half that we had the game in hand. Today, the best thing we have done, especially in the second half, was that we played with the rhythm we have to play. We cannot play all the time in one rhythm. In the right moment we have to run and today we did it really well. The most difficult position in football is the striker. You are surrounded by two players. The space is minimal and in front you have two or three holding midfielders. You are surrounded by five people. You don't have time. You have to be so smooth and good. He (Phil Foden) was a little bit impatient in the final third in the second half. He had to make the extra pass. If you don't see a clear shot, take one second more. But he fought and ran and pressed and helped us to have rhythm. When Phil, Bernardo and Kevin go in the first action so aggressive it is so addictive for the players behind. We can stay high and the second half was a perfect example of that.'

Post-match notes

Our star man against United was Kevin De Bruyne and this was a sensational performance by the skipper who was at the heart of everything good City did on the day. De Bruyne had been on top of his game for a while now and with two goals and an assist, this was the Belgian at his masterful best.

v Sporting CP
Wednesday, March 9

'IF MY PLAYERS KEEP SHOWING THE SAME FOCUS AND DEDICATION WE WILL BE THERE FIGHTING FOR TROPHIES'

UEFA Champions League

GOOD evening City fans and welcome back to the Etihad, so soon after our last game here.

Sunday was a fantastic occasion for us.

A derby is always such a big game for the fans – so much passion and emotion surrounds the match – but we managed it perfectly.

It's always important on those days to play our normal game, stick to our principles and not let the emotion affect us. We did that on Sunday, which was fantastic to see.

I was delighted with my players. Our display in the second half was excellent – defensively, offensively, commitment – we were exceptional.

I hope the fans enjoyed the game. I know how much it means to all of you, so I was delighted we were able to play so well and get the victory.

If my players keep showing the same focus and dedication from now until the end of the season, we will be there fighting for trophies.

But I understand how hard this league is. Everything is difficult and complicated. Our rivals are so, so good – all we can do is be professional, work hard and be the best we can be.

If we do that, we can be proud of our efforts no matter what happens.

There are ten games left and we know we will have to take almost all the points to be champions. That's how good our rival is. It is a huge challenge for us but one I know my players will do everything to achieve.

Now it's time for the Champions League again. We got a fantastic result in the first leg against Sporting, but nothing is finished.

The very best teams in Europe are in this competition and anything can happen at any time. My players know they have to fight for every ball and be the best they can be tonight if we want to be in the draw for the next phase.

I want to give a warm welcome to the Sporting players, staff and fans. We have watched so many Sporting games and they have become a really top team. It is a pleasure to be able to compete against them and test ourselves.

I want to finish by thanking you for your support. The noise on Sunday was incredible! We feel your support and it means so much.

Enjoy the game!

Manchester City 0, Sporting CP 0
(Manchester City win 5-0 on aggregate)

Line-up: Ederson (Carson 73), Egan-Riley, Stones, Laporte (Mbete 84), Zinchenko, Fernandinho, Gundogan, Bernardo (Mahrez 46), Jesus, Foden (McAtee 46), Sterling Subs not used: Slicker, Grealish, Rodrigo, De Bruyne, Kayky, Delap, Edozie.

Manchester City eased into the quarter-finals of the Champions League after closing out our last 16 tie against Sporting with a goalless draw in the second leg.

A professional job was all that was required of Pep Guardiola's men following our devastatingly clinical display in Lisbon three weeks ago and we duly delivered at the Etihad Stadium to progress to the last eight with a 5-0 aggregate victory.

The hosts were in complete control throughout what proved to be a low-key contest, with Gabriel Jesus' disallowed goal the closest either side came to scoring.

Pep's post-match reaction: 'The first half was better than the second. I think after the goal was disallowed we were not as active. We didn't make movements. It's not easy because after this [first leg] result it was already over. We should have played the second half like we did in the last four minutes. We didn't do it, but it's not easy after 5-0. I would say no (in wanting to avoid Premier League sides). It is difficult for us but for them too and for opposition from other countries. We are in the eight best teams in Europe and we will prepare well. Next Friday we'll see the draw and prepare. It's an honour to be there. Important teams are already out. We'll see what happens but already the four [English] teams (could be) in the last eight.'

Monday, March 14
Premier League
Crystal Palace 0, Manchester City 0

Line-up: Ederson, Walker, Stones, Laporte, Cancelo, Rodrigo,
De Bruyne, Bernardo, Grealish, Foden, Mahrez.
Subs not used: Steffen, Carson, Ake, Mbete, Fernandinho, Zinchenko,
Gundogan, Sterling, Jesus.

City were forced to settle for a share of the Premier League spoils as we were held to a goalless draw on a frustrating night at Selhurst Park.

Pep Guardiola's side did everything but score against Palace, with Joao Cancelo and Kevin De Bruyne both hitting the post in either half and Bernardo Silva twice coming within an ace of finding the target.

However, a well-drilled Eagles side managed to soak up all our pressure in what proved an action-packed encounter with both sides ultimately settling for a point in south London.

Pep's post-match reaction: 'We played a really good game.
Really good in a different stadium and against a difficult side.
They have quality to run. We lost the build-up ball, but it was
a really good game. We played a fantastic football game in all
departments. It was difficult to control their players up front. We
created a lot of chances. On another day we will score. Now

Pep Guardiola

we have four points and one game more (than second-placed
Liverpool). We've got to win a lot of games. There are still nine
games, a lot of points to go. We were not brilliant up front, but
in general it was a really good game. They know that when they
play like this there is nothing to say. We did everything. What
I want from my team is to do better than the opponent. We had
our chances and we couldn't convert. Sometimes it happens. I
thought a lot to make changes, but they were playing good. They
all had the ability to score goals. They were playing good. There
are many games to play still – we have to win a lot of games
still. The way we played there are no regrets. We prefer to win
of course but it was well played. We played to win the game.
We created more, conceded few, we played amazing in a difficult
stadium. We did a good game. We were 14 points ahead and
they (Liverpool) had two games less. They have one now. I said
many times that there are many games to play. We have to win
games. I'm going to watch the Champions League and then I'll
watch Liverpool (away to Arsenal) on Wednesday. Liverpool
is an interesting team to watch. Now we have five days before
Southampton.'

Post-match notes

The spectacular strikes that saw efforts from Joao
Cancelo and Kevin De Bruyne both cannon back off the
post remarkably meant that City had now hit the woodwork
on 19 occasions this season — that's three times more
than any other side.

Sunday, March 20
FA Cup quarter-final
Southampton 1, Manchester City 4

Goals: Sterling (12), De Bruyne (62), Foden (75), Mahrez (78)

Line-up: Steffen, Walker, Stones, Laporte (Ake 83), Cancelo (Zinchenko 83), Rodrigo (Fernandinho 83), Gundogan, De Bruyne, Grealish (Foden 63), Jesus (Mahrez 63), Sterling.
Subs not used: Carson, Bernardo.

Manchester City secured a place in the FA Cup semi-finals with a 4-1 win away at Southampton.

On a sun-drenched afternoon on the South Coast, Raheem Sterling gave City an early lead, only for Southampton to equalise on the stroke of half time when Aymeric Laporte deflected the ball into his own net.

But three second-half goals sealed a fine victory. Kevin De Bruyne fired home a penalty after Gabriel Jesus was fouled inside the box, before substitutes Phil Foden and Riyad Mahrez produced outstanding quality to ensure safe passage into the last four of the FA Cup for the fifth time in six seasons.

Pep's post-match reaction: 'We started really well and then we forgot to play. We know it's so difficult because Southampton are one of the best organised teams. It is so difficult. The second half was much better. We showed more personality. They had a chance with Adams but our quality made the difference. It's not a comfortable victory. They are a tough opponent and we know it. Now we go into international break and we are in three competitions. Every game is a final. We have a chance still to fight for the FA Cup. We are there. I think everyone needs a little bit of a break. It will be good to see new faces for a while on holiday this week. After we come back, we know what we have. We have the quarter-final of the Champions League, we have the Premier League, we have semi-finals of the FA Cup. The nice thing for the team is that fact. Arriving in the last weeks of the season we are there fighting for the titles. This is so nice. I would have smiled at the beginning of the season to be in front of you at this stage and to be in this position. How many times has it [the treble] happened in this country? Once. It is not easy. Hopefully, the players come back from the national team because it is tough to fight for many things. Now we have 15 days off and they'll arrive two days before they have play Burnley and then it's Liverpool and Atletico Madrid. Maybe one day UEFA can explain the reason why. It is what it is. It [the treble] is far, far away. It's better to think about Burnley first.'

Post-match notes

City had now scored four or more goals in a single match for the 80th time under Pep Guardiola in all competitions. The next most such games by an English club in this time is Liverpool's 58.

APR

2022

With the finishing line in sight, every game carried huge significance and although our hopes of FA Cup glory ended, we survived a bruising encounter to reach the Champions League semi-finals and remained in the Premier League box seat

2nd: Burnley (PL) A
5th: Atletico Madrid (CL) H
10th: Liverpool (PL) H
13th: Atletico Madrid (CL) A
16th: Liverpool (FAC) H
20th: Brighton & Hove Albion (PL) H
23rd: Watford (PL) H
26th: Real Madrid (CL) H
30th: Leeds United (PL) A

Saturday, April 2
Premier League
Burnley 0, Manchester City 2

Goals: De Bruyne (5), Gundogan (25)

Line-up: Ederson, Walker, Laporte, Ake, Cancelo, Rodrigo, Gundogan,
De Bruyne (Bernardo Silva 78), Grealish, Sterling, Foden (Jesus 64).
Subs not used: Steffen, Stones, Zinchenko, Fernandinho,
Mahrez, Egan-Riley, Mbete.

Manchester City returned to the top of the Premier League table after a brief hiatus with a 2-0 victory at Burnley.

Liverpool's 2-0 win at home to Watford in the day's early kick off had seen the Merseysiders move two points clear of City for a few hours, but our result at Turf Moor sees us move a point clear ahead of next week's showdown between the two sides at the Etihad.

Brilliant first-half goals from Kevin De Bruyne and Ilkay Gundogan sealed the three points.

Pep's post-match reaction: 'We came here to win the game and we did it. You never know what's going to happen after an international break. The pitch was difficult because the grass was so high but we adapted. The goal after five minutes was important but we still had to play 85 more. In the second half they pushed more, they went 4-4-2 and they were more aggressive. It was made more complicated by the fact we couldn't score the third goal. Being in a position to fight for the title is so nice – you want to arrive in April and May fighting for them. This is why we've fought for the last 10, 11 months. It's a busy week – first we'll think about Atletico Madrid and then after that we'll think about Liverpool. The players have to be ready, we look forward and see what we can do. Sometimes players who play ten minutes can win us the title. Of course, the players feel it but Liverpool feel it too. They know how hard we have fought and how tough the opponent is. We are now one point (ahead) but the way we played at Crystal Palace and Southampton we should be in a better position. We played awesome, we played much worse in FA Cup but won 4-1, you tell me the reason why? It's football. But I am proud and after five or six seasons winning, still we are there in the last stages of the season fighting for the title, that means we are a big club. Now the players know it, you lose, you lose the competition. They know it and they train like this and of course they feel it. But our opponents will feel it too. We have to feel the pressure that every game we play we can't lose. If we lose we can't win. We have to feel the pressure. We have to concentrate on Champions League, then have five days to prepare for Liverpool. Feel the pressure, live it and handle it or else we won't be champions.'

Post-match notes

This was Aymeric Laporte's 100th Premier League appearance and our victory took the total number of points he collected in that period to 254 — more than any other player has managed in their first 100 games in the competition. The win meant we were the only side yet to drop a point from a winning position in the Premier League this season, winning all 23 games in which we've led. No side has ever gone through an entire Premier League campaign without dropping points when ahead.

On the importance of his squad in the title run-in...

It's not necessary to tell you how important Ilkay is for us and for me personally, he has to compete with Kevin De Bruyne and Bernardo.

Bernardo was the best we have had this season and Kevin apart from little injuries has arrived in a good moment. Even Gabriel Jesus against Southampton, he made an assist and got the penalty that helped us to score the second goal.

His influence on the team, it doesn't matter when he plays, he had two shots on target and kept the ball, that is what we need.

The players have to be ready, we look forward and see what we can do. Sometimes players who play ten minutes can win us the title.

v Atletico Madrid
Tuesday, April 5

'I CANNOT ASK ANY MORE OF MY PLAYERS SO FAR AND IF THEY CONTINUE IN THE SAME WAY, WE HAVE A CHANCE'

UEFA Champions League

GOOD evening, everyone and welcome to the Etihad Stadium for this incredible occasion: a Champions League quarter-final against Atletico Madrid, one of the best teams in the world.

This is what we all love – big games on the biggest stage. I hope you are all as excited as I am.

Welcome to everyone who has travelled from Madrid – the fans, players and staff. And also to Diego Simeone, a manager I respect so much. He has created a team that is built in his image and how long he has been manager there says everything you need to know about the success he has had.

It is great to see a manager who commands so much respect – not just from his players and the fans, but from everyone inside the club. The players know he is the manager – he has authority and they follow him. This is why they have been so consistent for so long.

You cannot believe how tough an opponent Atletico Madrid will be over these two games. They will fight for absolutely everything and, believe me, we will have to be at our best to make it to the semi-finals.

It was great to return from the March international break with a win against Burnley. We have been preparing for these types of games for many years, so we knew how difficult it was going to be. We scored early on so that helped us a lot.

But the game is never finished until you score the

third or fourth, so we had to concentrate until the end.

We went there to win the game and we did it. You never know what's going to happen after an international break. The pitch was difficult because the grass was so high, but we adapted and played well.

When you arrive in May challenging to lift the title it means you have had an incredible season. Being here is because we work a lot and we have done that every single season. A lot of credit must go to the whole organisation.

We will fight now for the final two months of the season. I cannot ask any more of my players so far. If they continue in the same way from now until the end, we have a chance. That's all I can say. I am so proud of them.

Enjoy the game tonight and thank you for your support throughout this season.

Manchester City 1, Atletico Madrid 0

Goals: De Bruyne (70)

Line-up: Ederson, Cancelo, Stones, Laporte, Ake, De Bruyne, Rodrigo, Gundogan (Grealish 68), Mahrez (Foden 68), Silva, Sterling (Jesus 68).
Subs not used: Zinchenko, Steffen, Fernandinho, Carson, Egan-Riley, Mbete.

City will take a narrow but fully deserved 1-0 lead to

Madrid next week after a gruelling, hard-fought first leg at the Etihad.

The game played out exactly as predicted, with the visitors defending resolutely and City attacking almost from start to finish.

But one moment of magic from Phil Foden finally unlocked the Atleti defence for Kevin De Bruyne to slot home the only goal of the game.

Pep's post-match reaction: 'It was a difficult game against tough opponents – they played two banks of 5 for the first 25-30 minutes and it was so difficult to find spaces – but we were patient enough except for the first 10. The first 5-10 minutes of the second half we attacked not at the right rhythm and we didn't play the way we play. But yeah, it was a good result today. We had one or two more chances to score a second with Kevin, but good result and we won the game. In games like this we need a striker and they defend so well, so deep and compact and it is difficult to find spaces. We were patient because we have to win this type of game and not get anxious and nervous. They have incredible talent up front. If you are not attacking in the right way they can punish you. I don't know what to expect second leg.. It was different when it was 1-0, we were a little bit disorganised and they started to counter-attack and they have incredible quality up front and if you don't attack in the right way, they will punish you. For the second game, I try to expect what I expect of my team. I don't judge what they do are what they are going to do, because I don't know. It is not that I don't

*care, it's more the fact that, OK, we have a game with 1-0 –
after we went ahead we were a bit disjointed, the player started to
press a little bit higher, they had more combination. I guess what
happened in the last 15-20 minutes of the game will be how it
will be in Madrid. We have to prepare and adapt but we have
five days prepare to Liverpool and then we go there to try and
adapt a little bit better and go there to try and win the game.
We have to go through our emotions and do what we have to
do. There will be a referee there. We will prepare tactically and
mentally to play in a great stadium with an environment where
they have faced this situation many times – more than us. It will
be a good test for us on our maturity.'*

Pep Guardiola

**v Liverpool
Sunday, April 10**

'ON DAYS LIKE THIS, IT'S IMPORTANT TO PLAY WITH PERSONALITY – I WANT MY PLAYERS TO HAVE NO REGRETS'

Premier League

HELLO City fans, and thanks for being here at the Etihad again, just five days after our last match.

I was very pleased to get the win on Tuesday against Atletico Madrid, who are very tough opponents. It was a really hard 90 minutes because they make it so difficult to find spaces. But the most important thing is we won the game and we go to Madrid with a lead. At this stage of the competition, that is a huge positive for us.

All our thoughts have been focused on today's game, but once that is out of the way we will adapt a little bit and go to Spain and try to win the second leg.

In general, I have to say again how delighted I am with this group of players. I know I say it so often but it's because they deserve it. Sometimes on the side of the pitch I wave my arms and shout, but it's because I want the best for them.

Their attitude is fantastic and to be their manager honestly makes me so proud.

I want to welcome Jurgen Klopp and the Liverpool players, staff and fans here today. There is no doubt, today is a huge occasion for everyone. City and Liverpool have pushed one another really hard in the last five years and the consistency of both teams has been amazing. Both teams have raised the bar in terms of what it takes to win the Premier League. It is an honour to be here fighting for the title with them again.

They deserve huge credit for what they have done

since Jurgen took over. He is a top manager and I always love playing against his sides because I learn something new about this wonderful sport. But as a manager, you have to find solutions and that is what we will try to do today.

On days like this, it's always so important to play with personality. My players know what their strengths are, and I want them to give their all and have no regrets. If we do that, I am confident we can get a good result.

Hopefully everyone enjoys the game. These are the kind of occasions we all want be a part of. Your energy in the stands, as always, will be very important.

Thank you for your constant support.

Manchester City 2, Liverpool 2

Goals: De Bruyne (5), Jesus (36)

Line-ups: Ederson, Walker, Stones, Laporte, Cancelo, Rodrigo, De Bruyne, Bernardo, Jesus (Grealish 82), Foden, Sterling (Mahrez 75). Subs not used: Steffen, Ake, Gundogan , Zichenko, Fernandinho, McAtee, Lavia.

Manchester City remain in pole position in the Premier League after a thrilling top of the table clash with Liverpool ended in a 2-2 draw.

City made a flying start to a breathless encounter, opening the scoring in the sixth minute when Kevin De Bruyne capitalised on a quick free-kick to send a

20-yard effort past Alisson via a deflection off Joel Matip.

Diogo Jota managed to pull one back for the visitors, but the home side remained on the front foot, and De Bruyne hit the outside of the post with a shot on the turn before Gabriel Jesus arrived unmarked at the far post to lift Joao Cancelo's superb cross over Alisson and in off the crossbar to give us a deserved lead eight minutes before the interval.

Liverpool then stunned the hosts with an equaliser a minute into the second period as Sadio Mane fired emphatically past Ederson.

It was City who looked more dangerous in the closing stages, but both sides walked away with a point that maintains our advantage in the title race.

Pep's post-match reaction: 'It was a fantastic game from both sides. I have the feeling we missed opportunities to beat them, a feeling that we leave them alive. Heads up. I said to the team after the game, how good they have done, how proud we are. I think it was a good game for fans around the world. I am so happy with how we played. Normally when you do many many good things, you can understand why the sadness would be there. I said forget about it. We were ourselves. We performed incredibly well. We could not win but it's football. That can happen. I like that (Kevin De Bruyne) is a player who does not just make a lot of assists, he is scoring a lot. I told him he has to score more goals to reach another stage. He is scoring a lot of goals and making chances, knowing the position he is playing is so difficult against Liverpool because they are so narrow. And his vision for the last pass is exceptional. It's true he struggled in the first part of the season a lot with the injuries from the Champions League final and the European Championships. He has been at this level many times. The year we made 100 points at that level Kevin was incredible.'

Post-match notes

As he so often is, Kevin De Bruyne was the driving force in the City midfield, delivering a performance in which ingenuity and industry married to wonderful effect. It was De Bruyne who led the charge in the first half, when he was denied a second goal by the woodwork and he continued to dictate our attack after the break when he survived a series of robust challenges. De Bruyne's goal was his sixth in his last six appearances and his opener means he has now netted in four in a row in all competitions for the first time for the Club.

On continually learning and evolving as a manager...

What I see there are many things, I am close (to Jurgen) We are quite similar in many things, but in the final third they are more 'wow' for the quality of player they have, but I learn a lot not just from Jurgen, but also from every manager I see in the Premier League.

I'm curious to see the opponent what they do.

This is the reason why I am a manager, to discover the shape they are going to play, and see how we can control them and do it, it's the only reason why I'm here sitting in front of you – the only one.

It's too much work and stress sometimes and you see the players are sad because they don't play when they deserve to and you feel it's your responsibility, that's not good I don't like it but of course I learn many things.

That's why I feel a better manager now than when I started.

I learn from my opponents, I learn from reading books on tactics or whatever, the experience of what they do and have and next time try to do better against them and beat them next time.

On how Liverpool rivalry has made City better…
When you achieve 100 points and after 98 points, you need someone to push you from behind to make you realise they are there and they are close.

You have to make another step, that's for sure. I don't know what Liverpool is going to do but knowing the club and our chairman and CEO we want to grow and I am pretty sure we want to be there more years.

I am pretty sure Liverpool and other teams are going to try and do it as well. For both teams the most credit I give is the consistency through the years for many years. It is not winning one Premier League.

It has been five years every three days. That is what I am proud of most.

I will always remember the time here when I am retired and I will remember the biggest opponent was Liverpool.

I have been here five years and played many times. All the time we were close.

I faced Jurgen one year in Bayern Munich. Every season, except the year we made 100 points and they did 99 two seasons later, the rest it was tight.

Always we control each other because they are good and hopefully they think we are good too.

Wednesday, April 13
UEFA Champions League
Atletico Madrid 0, Manchester City 0
(Manchester City win 1-0 on aggregate)

Line-ups: Ederson, Walker (Ake 71), Stones, Laporte, Cancelo, Rodrigo,
Bernardo (Fernandinho 79), Gundogan, Mahrez,
De Bruyne (Sterling 65), Foden.
Subs not used: Steffen, Carson, Dias, Zinchenko,
Grealish, Delap, Edozie, McAtee, Lavia.

City booked our passage through to the Champions League semi-finals thanks to a hard fought goalless draw at Atletico Madrid in our quarter-final second leg.

In what was a compelling, fiercely fought encounter at a hostile Wanda Metropolitano Stadium, Ilkay Gundogan hit the post in what was a fine first half from Pep Guardiola's side.

However, City had to dig deep after the break in the face of a fiery Atletico onslaught as the hosts stepped up the pressure.

But we held firm and showed our composure, while Atletico were reduced to 10-men late on when Felipe was shown a second yellow card.

Ederson also produced two stunning saves deep into injury time as we deservedly progressed through to a last four meeting with Real Madrid 1-0 on aggregate thanks to last week's first leg triumph at the Etihad.

Pep's post-match reaction: 'Today we celebrate because it is the third time in Manchester City's history we are in the Champions League semi-finals. It is the champions of Spain and they played with energy and in second half were better than us and we were lucky we didn't concede. In the first half we had chances, overall we are in the semi-finals – it is well deserved. The opponent is so tough, all teams in the Champions League come here and suffer so it is important we go through. We defended everything. But if they had scored in the last action would the mental strength not be there? In this stadium in this competition it is always difficult. It is a big compliment for the players. We cannot expect every time to make everything marvellous. We have to suffer. I am proud because the opponent was really good. We tried to take the ball but were not able. With the people and chances, they had they could have scored a goal. They pushed us a lot, they were excellent second half. We forgot to play and we were in big, big trouble. They had chances to score, the second half we had just one. The first half was pretty good. They came out aggressively, we had one or two clear chances. In the second half of the second leg they were much better but at the same time we defended with everything. When a team plays like that we could not have the ball and our build-up was in danger. It is 1-0 in the UEFA Champions League, we are not used to being in this competition much.'

Saturday, April 16
FA Cup semi-final
Manchester City 2, Liverpool 3

Goals: Grealish (47), Silva (91)

*Line-up: Steffen, Cancelo, Stones, Aké, Zinchenko, Fernandinho,
Silva, Jesus (Mahrez 83), Grealish, Foden, Sterling.
Subs not used: Dias, Gundogan, Laporte, Rodrigo, De Bruyne,
Ederson, Delap, Lavia.*

Manchester City fell at the semi-final stage of the FA
Cup for the third consecutive season after a 3-2 defeat
to Liverpool at Wembley.

Liverpool were excellent in the opening period and
established a commanding half-time lead thanks to
Ibrahima Konate's header and a double from Sadio
Mane.

City improved after the break and scored almost
immediately after the restart through Jack Grealish –
and Bernardo Silva tapped home in stoppage time to
make it 3-2.

But Liverpool held on during a frantic period of
added time and they will face either Chelsea or Crystal
Palace in this year's showpiece final.

*Pep's post-match reaction: 'I want to learn from that and more
from the first half than the second. We will learn more from the*

first half in the future. For six months we are there, our team is good, our 11 players are good, we lost because our opponents were good, but we made a good comeback and gave everything, that's all you have to do. In the first half we couldn't do it for many reasons, the emotion of the game, the first action they arrive they score a goal and after the second goal, it's not easy to face Liverpool in these situations. At the end we defend the throw-in really poorly, they make a switch of play and score the third one. In the second half we did everything, in the end anything could happen in football, the second half was 3-0 and we react, we have to take the positive things from that. Now our psychology is seven games in the Premier League, we know exactly what we have to do to try to win the Premier League. Now we need to rest and recover the injuries and go game by game. We don't have time, Wednesday we have another match, then we have Watford, then we have Real Madrid and another one. We knew today if we win we continue to the final, if not, we lose the competition.'

Post-match notes

City's bid to win the FA Cup is over. Focus now is firmly fixed on winning the Premier League and Champions League, with a huge period of football still ahead of us. There are seven matches remaining in the Premier League and City are one point clear of Liverpool. There's little room for error, with every game carrying huge significance. Crucially, though, we are in the box seat.

v Brighton
Wednesday, April 20

'EVERY GAME PROVIDES SO MANY DIFFICULTIES – BUT WE'RE IN A GREAT POSITION TO ACHIEVE ALL WE WANT TO ACHIEVE'

Premier League

GOOD evening, everyone and welcome back to the Etihad for tonight's game against Brighton. Everyone knows they are a team that play really good football, so I am very excited to play against them. I like their style and respect Graham Potter so much.

As always, I want send a personal welcome to everyone connected to Brighton who has made the trip to Manchester – players, staff and fans. It should be a great occasion and I hope you enjoy your time here.

The Premier League is so tough because every single team has different qualities and every game provides so many difficulties. Tonight will be the same, so we have to be at our best. We know we have seven games left and if we win them all we are champions. It is seven cup finals for us, and they are all as important as each other.

There is no doubt this game comes after a very difficult period for us in terms of the number of fixtures, the importance of the matches and our travel schedule. To play Atletico, Liverpool, Atletico, Liverpool in a short space of time is difficult, but, overall, I am happy with my players' efforts. We are in a great position with only a few weeks left of the season left to play, so that means we are doing things the right way.

It is so hard for players to play so many high-intensity matches in a short space of time. Both physically and mentally, it can be draining. But my players have been exceptional. To play four matches that were so emotional, against two top teams, and do so many good things is a really good sign.

Saturday's result in the FA Cup semi-final was not what we wanted, but in the second half my players showed incredible pride. When you talk about being tired, in the second half we didn't look it. The first half was difficult, but to come out and play with personality like we did was very good.

I want them to continue doing all the things that have made us so successful over the last five years. We have our way of preparing and playing and we should stick to it. If we do that, I think we can have a successful end to the season.

One thing I know for sure is this: if we are to win trophies, we will need our fans behind us. Thank you for your support.

Manchester City 3, Brighton 0

Goals: Mahrez (53), Foden (65), Silva (82)

Line-up: Ederson, Cancelo, Stones (Zinchenko 77), Laporte, Ake (Dias 46), Rodrigo, Gundogan, De Bruyne, Mahrez, Bernardo, Foden. Subs not used: Steffen, Sterling, Jesus, Grealish, Fernandinho, Palmer, Lavia.

Manchester City returned to winning ways and the top of the Premier League with a comfortable victory over Brighton and Hove Albion at the Etihad Stadium.

Pep Guardiola's side bounced back from our FA Cup semi-final defeat to Liverpool with a 3-0 win that restores our one-point lead over Jurgen Klopp's men, who temporarily took pole position following their 4-0 thrashing of Manchester United on Tuesday.

After a frustrating first half, our patience was rewarded after the break when Riyad Mahrez and Phil Foden both scored via deflections, before Bernardo Silva sealed the three points with a precise finish that confirmed Guardiola's 250th win as City boss.

Pep's post-match reaction: 'The way we defended was good. Today we were so dynamic, we were so aggressive without the ball. Before we could not do it for many reasons, we were mentally fatigued in the last games. If you want to make this step you have to come back to those terms and the defence will help us to do that. Today they were brilliant. The people will see that. They will seem the team were alive. They pressed to regain the ball and after the transitions with Kevin, Bernardo and Phil, we did it. In the first half we didn't concede a lot. In the second half in the first three or four minutes after kick-off we didnt take the ball but once we arrived there we were so aggressive in the final third and in the end we found the goals. That feeling is there. If we win all the games we will be the champions. If we drop points we won't. Today we came back against a side who won away against Tottenham and Arsenal. They are a quality team, with a system and set up really well. We were so aggressive and we had contact with Kevin and we could run.

We were patient and in the second half we found a goal. I don't think the first half and second half were too different, but we found a goal in the second half. Now three more days and Watford. Liverpool are one of the best sides in football history. We are facing one of the best sides ever. That's why being there means a lot after winning Premier Leagues in the past. The players know it. We have faced them, we know. Unfortunately, we could not win against them but I would not change much With (a four-point advantage) we could drop one action, but now we cannot drop anything. We have been in this position. We play against ourselves, our action, our nerves. It is difficult, but at the same time I am sure the players will make the step. Maybe in five weeks we are able to reach the final of Champions League, but in the Premier League, it is just one month. It is not easy, but at the same time we will fight. We were 11 months here together for just one month. We are going to have to give everything. In your body and your mind and your private life, to give our best.'

Post-match notes

It was a landmark night for Kevin De Bruyne as he clocked up a triple century of appearances in a sky-blue shirt and he ensured he would remember the milestone fondly with a typically influential performance. The 30-year-old looked the most likely to make something happen as City struggled to make the breakthrough in the first half and, when it arrived, it was as a result of his powerful surging run. Another classy and tireless display from a player who is in excellent form at a critical moment in the campaign.

On staying calm in the season's run-in...

I have the feeling they're calm during the days and in the moment of the game, they have the right tension to do it, especially in the Premier League.

The Champions League is a different competition – the emotions are more sensitive. I don't know the right word to use to explain.

The Champions League is completely different but in the Premier League, you have just one option – all of us know it – to win the game. There are not many interpretations of what you have to do.

The most important thing with six games left, the most important job is done: to qualify for the Champions League.

I said many times: you take it for granted. City, for the last nine or ten years, it's happened but it is so difficult to do it, especially with six games left. Liverpool and ourselves have done an incredible job.

When it's nine or ten years with Roberto [Mancini] and Manuel [Pellegrini] we always qualify, the structure was there before we arrived. We continue to do that especially with the Premier League and cups, and in the Champions League consistently arriving to the end and fighting for them. We are going to do it again.

When I qualify for the Champions League, I get a hug and a kiss! I know how important it is for many reasons. For managers and staff and players to play in the Champions League, it is so important.

It's not speculation. We just have to win the game… How? I'd love to tell you but I don't know. We have to be constant: don't do unnecessary mistakes in our box and be consistent.

Be consistent and the game will be okay because we play well.

We are who we are and will go to the last drop of energy in our body and mind, I am sure of that. I know the guys and myself, I try to find the right words and body language to let them feel it's the last."

On being in the position of fighting for titles…
Of course we enjoy it. We'd prefer to be in this position than not, having the chance to try to make back to back titles.

I love it. Fighting for knockout stages, every game is important and decisive. It means we've done good things before – otherwise we wouldn't be here.

Being there to play in the Champions League semi-finals and league arriving at the end fighting is a joy, a pleasure. Now we try to do it.

You don't often have chance to make back-to-back titles. After the game (against Brighton last Wednesday), like I said it remains six games.

We've already qualified for the Champions League which is a big success and now we have the target of the Premier League.

Pep Guardiola

v Watford
Saturday, April 23

'THE EQUATION IS SIMPLE: WIN ALL OUR GAMES AND WE WILL BE CHAMPIONS. IT IS A PRIVILEGE TO BE IN THIS POSITION'

Premier League

HELLO City fans! I want to start by thanking you all for your support here on Wednesday when we played Brighton. We felt how close you were to us. When we have this feeling that you are there pushing us to win, it makes us better. The players can feel it and I can feel it. We will need you so much in the final weeks of the season, believe me.

I was very pleased with how we played against Brighton, a team who have been so difficult for their opponents this season. We were patient, defended well and were very dynamic in our attacks in the second half. We were so aggressive in the final third and we created chances. To win 3-0 against a top team makes me very, very happy. The players deserve huge credit.

We know the equation is simple: if we win all of our games, we will be champions. People have asked me about pressure and, of course, there is always pressure in football. But it is a privilege to be in this position. Every single team in world football wants to be there fighting for titles when the season gets towards the end. Manchester City in the last five, six seasons are always there, so we should be really proud of that.

I have told my players to keep playing the only way we know how. I want them to be brave and show personality. It's been the basis for the success we have had in the last years, and I see no reason to change this now.

We are going to give absolutely everything we have, I can promise you that.

Today we play Watford and I want to welcome Roy Hodgson, his players, staff and all the Watford fans. Roy is someone who has the respect of not just me but everyone in football. What he has achieved over such a long career is absolutely remarkable. The way he has remained fresh, always bringing new ideas, is something special.

And the thing you always know when you play one of Roy's teams is that they will be organised, fight for every ball and make life hard. Today will be no exception.

We have six 'cup finals' left in the Premier League to be champions. It will be so, so tough but we are ready. Thank you, once again, for your continued support. I hope we can make you proud.

Enjoy the game!

Manchester City 5, Watford 1

Goals: Jesus (4, 23, 49 pen, 53), Rodrigo (34)

Line-up: Ederson, Cancelo, Dias, Laporte (Ake 63), Zinchenko, Rodrigo (Mahrez 70), Fernandinho, De Bruyne (Gundogan 56), Grealish, Jesus, Sterling
Subs not used: Steffen, Bernardo, Foden, Egan-Riley, Mbete, Palmer.

Gabriel Jesus scored four and assisted a superb Rodri volley as Manchester City moved four points clear at the top of the Premier League table thanks to a 5-1 win over Watford at the Etihad.

The result means City's lead at the top of the Premier League table is extended to four points and it leaves us knowing five more wins will seal another Premier League title.

Pep's post-match reaction: 'Tonight I'll go home. We play on Wednesday so I'll start to think about Real Madrid. Tonight I'll watch some minutes from some games I want to watch, and that's all. The victory against Brighton gave us the opportunity to play another 'final' today, and the victory today gave us an opportunity to play another final against Leeds between the Madrid games. It's no more complicated than that. The situation hasn't changed today. We have to win all the games to be champions. We have five left. They're difficult ones because they're mixed in between the Champions League, but it's a pleasure and I'm so proud again to be here.'

Post-match notes

City are now the first team in Premier League history to win 15 consecutive matches against the same opponent. And Gabriel Jesus became the first player to score four goals in a single Premier League game since Tottenham's Son Heung-min vs Southampton in September 2020.

Pep Guardiola

v Real Madrid
Tuesday, April 26

'WE MUST ENJOY IT AND GIVE EVERYTHING WE HAVE IN OUR SOUL. IF WE DO THAT, WE HAVE A CHANCE'

UEFA Champions League

WELCOME to the Etihad for what should be a really special night.

Games don't come much bigger than this one. A Champions League semi-final against a team who has won this competition 13 times – I am so excited, and I am sure all of you are too.

I want to welcome everyone who has travelled from Madrid. And a special welcome to Carlo Ancelotti, a manager I respect so much.

He has managed so many special teams and won so many titles. He is a legend who will always be remembered for what he has achieved and the football his teams have played. It's an honour to be able to play against him again, and to do it in the semi-final of this beautiful competition makes it even more special.

Everybody knows how good Real Madrid are. They have quality in every single area of the pitch. They have shown in their previous rounds, they are very capable of hurting teams. We have to be ready but I trust my players.

The most important thing on nights like this is to make sure we play our game. We have to show personality and we have to stick to the principles that have been there for the past five years. This is the club's third Champions League semi-final and we must enjoy it and give everything we have in our soul. If we do that, we have a chance and we will leave the pitch with no regrets.

Pep Guardiola

I really enjoyed Saturday's win over Watford. I was pleased with the quality we showed and the result was exceptional.

That victory means we have the chance to play another 'final' against Leeds United on Saturday. This is the way we are thinking in the Premier League. One game at a time, and if we win, we get the chance to play another 'final'. It's that simple.

We have to win all the games to be champions. We have five left. They're difficult ones because they're mixed in between the Champions League, but it's a pleasure and I'm so proud again to be here.

I have said it a lot in recent weeks, but I really mean it: the support you guys have been giving us is making a difference. You have been amazing, and it really helps. The players feel it and are inspired by you, so thank you. Stay with us because it could be a very exciting few weeks.

Enjoy this evening's game!

Manchester City 4, Real Madrid 3

Goals: De Bruyne (2), Jesus (11), Foden (53), Silva (74)

Line-up: Ederson, Stones (Fernandinho 36), Zinchenko, Dias, Laporte, Rodrigo, De Bruyne, Bernardo, Foden, Mahrez, Jesus (Sterling 83). Subs not used: Aké, Gundogan, Grealish, Steffen, Carson, Egan-Riley, Mbete, Palmer, McAtee, Lavia.

City and Real Madrid produced a Champions League semi-final few who witnessed it will ever forget.

City will take a slender lead to Spain after winning the first leg 4-3, with more of the same likely in eight days' time.

City held a two-goal advantage on three separate occasions, thanks to goals from Kevin De Bruyne, Gabriel Jesus, Phil Foden and Bernardo Silva, but were pegged back each time by a Real Madrid side who refused to buckle on the night, with an inspired Karim Benzema scoring twice and Vinicius Junior grabbing his team's second.

Pep's post-match reaction: 'It was a good game of football, both teams have an incredible amount of quality players on the pitch with incredible personality to play. The result is what it is, we won and now we rest and then it's Leeds and we are going to travel to Spain next week and try and do a good result. To win this competition, from my experience, is that you have to overcome situations that football gives you. It was a fantastic game for both sides. We did many good things. Unfortunately, we conceded goals and we could not score more. But two games and we have another one in one week. We played a fantastic game against an incredible team. The moments where they rise and come back into the game in the first half I think we gave them as our build-up was so nervous. Normally we are so safe and so good. Also they press really good and strong. All around the world and for Manchester City, we are so proud. But it is about reaching the final and sometimes football happens. The result could have been better, and you have to perform really well over two games and we've performed really well in the first one. It's a good test to show the personality of our team and we travel there to try and win the game. I'm not going to complain about the result and I'm not going to complain about the performance – nothing. I am so proud and so incredibly happy at the way we performed. We did everything we could to win and had courage with and without the ball. Now we recover and hopefully arrive quite well for Leeds and then head to Madrid.'

Post-match notes

At 21, Phil Foden is the second English player to score a Champions League semi-final goal before turning 22. His goal came in a game in which Real Madrid conceded twice in the opening 11 minutes of a Champions League match for the first time in their history.

Saturday, April 30
Premier League
Leeds 0, Manchester City 4

Goals: Rodrigo (13), Ake (54), Jesus (78), Fernandinho (93)

Line-up: Ederson, Joao Cancelo, Dias, Laporte,
Ake (Zinchenko 60), Rodrigo (Fernandinho 83), Gundogan,
Grealish, Foden (Silva 80), Sterling, Gabriel Jesus.
Subs not used: Steffen, De Bruyne, Mahrez,
Egan-Riley, Mbete, McAtee.

City ensured Liverpool's stay at the Premier League summit was brief following a hard-earned but ultimately comfortable 4-0 victory over Leeds United.

The home side gave as good as they got in a physical, high-octane War of the Roses, but City gradually took control with goals from Rodrigo, Nathan Ake, Gabriel Jesus and Fernandinho sealing victory.

Pep's post-match reaction: 'We knew coming here the way they play, we suffered a lot in the first half. But in the end we had control and could have scored more. An incredible result for us. They are so fast up front. Today was so important to make our chances to be champions again. We defended well and sometimes these type of games set-pieces become so important. With Nathan Ake on the pitch, we are so strong. What a game Laporte played, he is doing an incredible season. We started really well but didn't expect five in the back and we were surprised but after the goal we suffered a lot, we conceded transitions. But after second goal from Ake, we created a lot of chances and so ahead of the Champions League second leg, this is a really good result I think the scoreline was more comfortable than it really was but I couldn't expect differently. We tried to put away what happened against Real Madrid and focus on the Premier League, fighting. We responded so well, defended well – Aymeric, Ruben, Gundo were fantastic. Sterling was so aggressive. I try to involve everyone and they did really well. Since I arrived in England, I heard about Elland Road – last year it was behind closed doors, today I experienced it and why it's so special. Fighting to stay in the Premier League – singing, chanting and how the people get behind them. Leeds is one of greatest teams in England, and I have sympathy for the fans. I said today it would be hard. We stuck together and in the end it's important to close that (goal difference) gap a little more. We have five games to go, potentially six until the end of the season. I prefer to feel less pressure than I am feeling. It is a long season and this is the last effort. It's in our hands. Wolves, Newcastle, West Ham and Aston Villa. We win (them all and) we will be champions – we drop points Liverpool will be champions. We know exactly what we need to do – win our games. Still it is a privilege and an honour to try win back to back titles and four Premier Leagues in five years. Right now it's not too much complicated, they are going to win their games.'

MAY

2022

And so a season that would ultimately include 58 games came to a thrilling climax. It wasn't to be in the Champions League, but, using that pain to good effect and with Liverpool pushing us all the way, a three-goal burst in five final day minutes bought the Premier League title home in front of a delirious Etihad Stadium

4th: Real Madrid (CL) A
8th: Newcastle United (PL) H
11th: Wolverhampton Wanderers (PL) A
15th: West Ham United (PL) A
22nd: Aston Villa (PL) H

Wednesday, May 4
UEFA Champions League
Real Madrid 3, Manchester City 1
(Real Madrid win 6-5 on aggregate)

Goal: Mahrez (73)

Line-up: Ederson, Walker (Zinchenko 72), Dias, Laporte, Cancelo,
Rodrigo (Sterling 94), De Bruyne (Gundogan 72), Bernardo, Foden,
Jesus (Grealish 79), Mahrez (Fernandinho 84).
Subs not used: Steffen, Carson, Ake, Fernandinho, Egan Riley,
Palmer, McAtee, Lavia.

City suffered Champions League semi-final heartbreak as Real Madrid staged a stunning late fightback to clinch a 3-1 second leg win after extra time at the Bernabeu to clinch a 6-5 win on aggregate.

Riyad Mahrez, the goal hero in last year's semi-final against Paris Saint-Germain, looked to have delivered again when he struck to give City a 73rd minute lead to put us 5-3 ahead on the tie.

But in a dramatic and gut-wrenching finale, Real substitute Rodrygo struck twice inside injury time to stun City and so send the tie into extra time.

And a 94th minute penalty from Karim Benzema sealed the most improbable of comebacks from the Spanish champions to break City's hearts.

Pep's post-match reaction: 'It is tough for us. We cannot deny it. We were so close to arriving in the Champions League final. We didn't play much good in the first half. We didn't find our game, but it's normal in this competition. The second half was much better. After the goal we controlled it. We found the game, we arrived at the byline. Jack (Grealish) helped us to control the game and unfortunately he could not finish when we were close. Before the first goal [for Madrid] we had two chances, especially one so clear with Jack. In that moment we didn't have the feeling we were in trouble for the way they attack. It didn't happen. They score a goal at the end. They have done it many times in their history. They put a lot of players in the box. Four strikers plus Militao and they find the goals. I have had defeats in the Champions League. I have had tough defeats with Barcelona against Chelsea when both games were exceptional and we could not reach the final. We need time now. One or two days, but we will rise. We will come up. We have to do it, with our people.'

On using Champions League pain to good effect...

We were close and could not do it. The players wanted to play again in the final of the Champions League.

But for this club to compete against Real Madrid was a joy. Don't forget how well we played a week ago here. But we could not do it.

For us it is an honour. Maybe it is not enough, but for me it is remarkable to be in the semi-final of the Champions League again after last season and played the way we did home and away against a great team.

I have to handle this. It's not about that…in the Premier League again we are there, FA Cup semi-finals again. Carabao Cup four times in a row.

This is what the club wants to be. This is why they seduce me to come here

People in sport know how difficult everything is but I accept it. We are sad… of course we are sad.

But now I am thinking only about Newcastle. That's enough focus.

This is the only concern I have and then after that Wolves and then West Ham. That's what is in my mind.

On the title race pushing City to be the best they can be…

The Premier League, I have said many times (it's about) the work you do every day.

A father and mother wake up every morning to go to work to bring food at home for the kids to grow up and go to school. This is the Premier League.

It's (about) consistency, every day, every day and I like it a lot.

Especially because we have been fighting an extraordinary team for the past three or four years.

I think that hopefully we push them and they push us to be our best and to our limits. Being there (fighting for the Premier League) is great – it's fantastic.

May 2022

**v Newcastle
Saturday, May 8**

'TO STILL BE FIGHTING FOR THE TITLE MEANS WE'VE DONE A LOT OF GOOD THINGS AND WE SHOULD ALL BE VERY PROUD'

Premier League

GOOD afternoon, everyone. It's a pleasure to be back here at the Etihad Stadium after two away games.

Our win at Leeds was very good. We created a lot of chances and played some excellent football. Of course, Wednesday in Madrid was very tough for us. We were close to reaching the Champions League final again and we were all disappointed we could not do it. But now we are back here with our people, and we must focus on the Premier League. We still have an incredible opportunity in front of us and we must do everything we can to take it.

As I said last time I wrote to you, our situation in the Premier League is very simple. We have four matches left and we need to win them all to be champions.

I know it makes every game so pressured for you as fans – we feel it too – but it's honestly such a pleasure for us to be in this situation. We are fighting an amazing rival in the toughest league in the world, but we are there with a chance of winning the title with just a few weeks left. That means we have done a lot of good things this season and we should all be very proud.

Today it's Newcastle, a team everyone knows is so dangerous right now because of their recent results. Eddie Howe has had a huge impact since taking over and deserves so much credit. Not only has he managed to get excellent results, you can also see his ideas have been accepted by the players. Clearly, he has the respect of everyone at Newcastle and to do that in such a short time is really good.

I want to welcome Eddie and his staff here today. And I also want to extend a really warm welcome to the Newcastle fans, who are always so good whenever we have been to St James' Park. Newcastle is an historic club, so this is a fixture I always look forward to.

When a team comes into a game in good form, you always have to be aware. The Newcastle players are happy, feel good, trust the manager's process and have confidence. That is a dangerous combination. My players know this, and we have been working since the Real Madrid match to ensure we can combat their threat.

Please remember how important your support is to us. The noise you make in the stadium drives us on – and we can feel your energy. I am not just saying this, guys, it's really true. All the players and staff feel it and it inspires us to be better.

Thank you and enjoy today's game.

Manchester City 5, Newcastle 0

Goals: Sterling (19, 83), Laporte (38), Rodrigo (61), Foden (90)

Line-up: Ederson, Cancelo, Zinchenko, Dias (Fernandinho 46), Laporte (Egan-Riley 87), Rodrigo, Gundogan, De Bruyne, Grealish, Sterling, Jesus (Foden 64).
Subs not used: Steffen, Ake, Bernardo, Mahrez, Mbete, Palmer.

City bounced back from the midweek disappointment against Real Madrid to thrash Newcastle United 5-0 and move three points clear of Liverpool at the top of the Premier League.

First-half goals from Raheem Sterling and Aymeric Laporte put us firmly in command against lively opposition.

Rodrigo bagged the third on the hour, before crucial late goals from Phil Foden and Sterling wrapped up a wonderful afternoon for the defending champions who now move within seven points of the title.

Pep's post-match reaction: 'I am very pleased. (It was a) perfect afternoon. Before the start of the game I felt in our crowd that they were disappointed, but not sad about who we are as a team and what we have done in the last five years every three days. Three more points. Three games left and one competition to play and big problems behind because we have just three defenders for these three games. We are going to try and do it. Now after what happened with Liverpool and with us today, Wednesday became a final. It is an absolute final and I am pretty sure we will prepare well to try and beat them. Sometimes I say to the players, you have to play good to lift the fans to let the opponent know here is not a nice place to come. Today we didn't need to do that. The people know these guys do it every three days for five years like today. They deserve it. They are one of the best groups I have ever had in my life as a manager, even as a player. It is an important three points after Liverpool and Tottenham (drew

1-1), but anything can happen in football. If it can happen in 56 seconds in Madrid, it can happen in three games.'

Post-match notes

City have scored five or more goals in the Premier League for the 30th time under Pep Guardiola — more than Liverpool (14) and Spurs (13). Kevin De Bruyne has been involved in 16 goals in his last 17 Premier League appearances, scoring nine and assisting seven, while Rodrigo has scored six goals in 30 Premier League appearances this term, equalling his combined total in his two previous seasons across 69 games.

Pep Guardiola

Wednesday, May 11
Premier League
Wolves 1, Manchester City 5

Goals: De Bruyne (7, 16, 24, 60), Sterling (84)

*Line-up: Ederson, Cancelo, Fernandinho (Mahrez 76),
Laporte (Ake 61), Zinchenko, Rodrigo, Gundogan, De Bruyne, Silva,
Foden (Grealish 81), Sterling.
Subs not used: Steffen, Mbete, Egan-Riley, Lavia, Palmer, Jesus.*

Kevin De Bruyne scored four goals as City thrashed Wolves 5-1 to move within four points of the Premier League title.

City's midfield maestro had completed his hat-trick with just 24 minutes on the clock, added another on the hour and Raheem Sterling scored a late fifth to cap a memorable night in the Black Country.

Only a coat of paint denied De Bruyne a fifth as he rattled the post in the dying moments in what was a superb victory for City.

Pep's post-match reaction: 'The way Kevin is playing in the last two or three months has been outstanding. I am so disappointed in him that he missed a fifth goal when he hit the post! He has always been a guy who is so generous and has the sense to make an assist, but I think this season he has the sense to be prolific and score goals. He won the game against Chelsea; he scored a goal against Madrid and has been scoring decisive goals. I am very pleased for him. Scoring four goals in the decisive part of the season right now is so important. You have to arrive in the box. You have to be close to the box and this season I think he has done that better and better. Hopefully, that can continue. Not just this year, but for the rest of his career. I have the feeling he has now started enjoying goals. Before it was just assists, but now I have the feeling he thinks "I like when my team-mates come to hug me because I scored a goal". It's good! We were exceptional. We made a really good performance. We played really well in this stadium; we know how difficult it is. (There are) two weeks left, it was a brilliant performance from all the players. All of them. They implemented our movement perfectly and made good runs for the people up front. We were good. It's an important victory. We need four points to be champion and we are going to try and get the first three on Sunday. We could have scored more. It is not about that because if we win our games goal difference is not important. We have a really tough game on Sunday, and we have incredible problems in (defence). We don't have players and against Antonio, Bowen, Lanzini, it will not be easy. But at the same time, it doesn't matter what happens, we are going to find a solution and we are going to go there to win the game.'

Post-match notes

Kevin De Bruyne's 17-minute hat-trick was the third fastest in Premier League history from the start of a game. City's third goal against Wolves made Pep Guardiola's side the top scorers of all Europe's top five major leagues so far this season.

Pep Guardiola

Sunday, May 15
Premier League
West Ham 2, Manchester City 2

Goals: Grealish (49), Coufal (69 og)

Line-up: Ederson, Cancelo, Fernandinho, Laporte, Zinchenko, Rodrigo,
De Bruyne, Bernardo, Mahrez, Jesus, Grealish.
Subs not used: Steffen, Ake, Sterling, Gundogan, Foden, Egan-Riley,
Mbete, Palmer, Lavia.

Manchester City staged a superb second half fightback to rescue a point against West Ham United which keeps our fate in the Premier League title race in our own hands heading into the final game of the season.

Jarrod Bowen's brace saw the Hammers open up a two-goal lead at half-time, but City came roaring back after the break thanks to a Jack Grealish volley and Vladimir Coufal's own goal.

Pep Guardiola's men might have taken all three points, only for Lukasz Fabianski to deny Riyad Mahrez from the penalty spot five minutes from time after Craig Dawson tripped Gabriel Jesus.

Pep's post-match reaction: 'It was a really good game. I think we played more than decent in the first half. Chances were so difficult to attack them. Very pleased to come back against West

Ham like we did in this stadium. The transition with Antonio is so difficult to control and in two uncertain balls, it looks like nothing is happening, they put a ball in behind, Bowen gets it really well and finished. We scored an early goal and had a really good second half. A point that we gained. West Ham away after an exceptional performance against Wolves – we knew it – we needed four points – and now there is no debate about goal difference, and no debate about anything, we just have to win our game and if we don't, Liverpool will be champions. I can assure you of something – in one week our stadium will be sold out, we will give them our lives and they will give theirs, all together. To do this is an incredible privilege, after many years together. It is incredible. To have our chance with our people, to win one game to be champions. I'm looking forward to it. We are going to rest for two days, mentally disconnect and then we are going to train for three or four days and prepare for the game on Sunday. It will be tough, emotional and we have to analyse what we have to do to beat Aston Villa, but we will give everything that we have for 95 minutes to win, I'm pretty sure of that… everything that we have.'

Post-match notes

This is the first time City have come back from two goals down in a top-flight game since 2012.

**v Aston Villa
Sunday, May 22**

'THIS IS THE MOMENT WE CAN BE PREMIER LEAGUE CHAMPIONS AND WE HAVE TO FEEL YOU THERE. LET'S DO IT TOGETHER!'

Premier League

HELLO everyone and welcome to the Etihad Stadium for the final game of the season.

We welcome Aston Villa here today. Steven Gerrard is a Premier League and England legend and someone who has brought so much to football, both as a player and now as a manager. I am delighted to welcome him here today, along with his staff, the Villa fans and their directors.

How many times in our more than one hundred years of history have we lived what we are going to live this afternoon all together? How many? At Brighton three years ago? The historical Sergio 93.20 moment? Paul Dickov at Wembley in 99…. Yes.. a few times in our lives.

Dear friends, there is just one thing we are not allowed to do this afternoon: we must not fail to enjoy this moment. We will regret it forever if we are not here as one.

In our last games at home against Real Madrid and Newcastle, we felt you so, so much. Against Real Madrid, even when they scored goals, all of you stayed with us and gave us the feeling we could win the game. And we did it. We want to listen to your breath, your passion, your laughs, from before the kick off until the end. Every second, moment, action, dribble, save, pass, goal. I want to feel you alive, non-stop. We want loud, loud and loud. Right?

We have a job to do, and we must do it as a collective. We simply have to win. We don't have any alternative but to win. We have to feel you with us on the pitch for the whole 95 minutes – it will help us, believe me. This is not about us being on the pitch and all of you are off the pitch. No. This afternoon will be all of us ON THE PITCH.

THIS IS THE MOMENT WE CAN BE PREMIER LEAGUE CHAMPIONS AND WE HAVE TO FEEL YOU THERE! LET'S DO IT TOGETHER.

To be in our stadium – with all of you – and have the chance to win the Premier League title in our own hands is a privilege and something very special. We should enjoy these moments as much as we can. As a club, these situations are relatively new. Embrace it and enjoy today as much as you can.

I have the feeling every year that winning the Premier League is harder. We have consistently been there fighting to win it, which says everything about the mentality and quality of my players.

It is an honour to manage these players. In football, you cannot be perfect, but this squad has shown so many times over the past five or six years how good they are. They really, really care about this club and want to win, always. You should all be really proud of them

Enjoy today's game. Thank you, once again, for your constant support this season in our home games – and especially when we play away. Without all of you – every single one of you – we could not be here on this privileged day that we are going to live in few minutes time.

Don't forget it: LOUD LOUD LOUD.

Manchester City 3, Aston Villa 2

Goals: Gundogan (76, 81), Rodrigo (78)

Line-up: Ederson, Stones, Laporte, Fernandinho (Zinchenko 45), Cancelo, Rodrigo, De Bruyne, Bernardo (Gundogan 69), Foden, Jesus, Mahrez (Sterling 56).
Subs not used: Carson, Walker, Ake, Grealish, Palmer, McAtee.

City staged another incredible final day fightback, scoring three goals in five second half minutes to dramatically beat Aston Villa 3-2 and so retain the Premier League title at a spellbound Etihad.

Having gone 2-0 down midway through the second half Pep Guardiola's side looked to be in danger of losing the crown to Liverpool, who beat Wolves 3-1

However, in amazing scenes reminiscent of our first Premier League triumph 10 years ago, with the same uncanny scoreline, we staged the most unbelievable of comebacks to seize the crown, as a brace from substitute Ilkay Gundogan and a Rodrigo strike lifted the lid off the Etihad.

It was a fightback full of grit and character and one

worthy of any title-winning side. And it meant we retained the crown, secured a fourth title in five years under Pep Guardiola and handed departing Club captain Fernandinho the perfect emotional send off.

Pep's post-match reaction: 'The last game is always special, a lot of emotions. The moment we scored the goal it changed everything. I told them it is normal, but you have to handle it. Oleks gave us a lot in the second half. We scored the goal and got the momentum and our fans did the rest. It was the best atmosphere I have lived since I came here. Tomorrow we can celebrate together in the Manchester streets with cigars and beers. Ilkay Gundogan is the best runner in second positions that we have. We arrive in the sides with Joao and Oleks. And we have people with the sense of tempo in the final third- but he is the best. We are legends. When you win four titles in five years then it's because these guys are so special. We will be remembered. We won with 100 points, second one at Brighton, winning at home with our people is the best. Four Premier Leagues in five years is probably the best achievements we have done in our careers. I've never seen a team like Liverpool in my life. I know it's tough, but they helped us become a better team season by season. We want to win. I have the feeling that the rivals are tough and they will be more tough next season. The moment we scored and equalised quickly we had a feeling that we had the chance to score the third. Today I have no energy to think about next season. We are champions again! We will defend our crown again and again.'

SEASON
STATISTICS

**The numbers that sum up the long and
successful season Pep Guardiola and his
team steered City to**

Season statistics

Appearances (all competitions)

Name	PL	FA	LC	Europe	Total
Joao Cancelo	36	5	1	9	51
Bernardo Silva	35	3	0	11	49
Ederson	37	1	0	11	49
Raheem Sterling	30	3	2	12	47
Riyad Mahrez	28	4	2	12	46
Rodrigo	33	2	0	10	45
Kevin De Bruyne	30	2	2	10	45
Phil Foden	28	4	2	11	45
Aymeric Laporte	33	2	0	9	44
Ilkay Gundogan	27	4	1	10	42
Gabriel Jesus	28	4	1	8	41
Ruben Dias	29	2	0	8	39
Jack Grealish	26	4	1	7	38
Fernandinho	19	4	1	8	32
Kyle Walker	20	3	1	7	31
Oleksandr Zinchenko	15	4	1	8	28
John Stones	14	4	1	8	27
Nathan Ake	14	5	1	6	26
Cole Palmer	4	1	2	3	10
Zack Steffen	1	4	2	1	8
James McAtee	2	2	1	1	6
Ferran Torres	4	0	1	0	5
Luke Mbete	0	1	1	1	3
CJ Egan-Riley	1	0	1	1	3
Liam Delap	1	1	0	1	3
Romeo Lavia	0	1	1	0	2
Kayky	1	1	0	0	2
Benjamin Mendy	1	0	0	0	1
Scott Carson	0	0	0	1	1
Josh Wilson-Esbrand	0	0	1	0	1
Finley Burns	0	0	1	0	1

Goals (all competitions)

Name	PL	FA	LC	Europe	Total
Riyad Mahrez	11	4	2	7	24
Kevin De Bruyne	15	1	1	2	19
Raheem Sterling	13	1	0	3	17
Phil Foden	9	1	1	3	14
Bernardo Silva	8	2	0	3	13
Gabriel Jesus	8	1	0	4	13
Ilkay Gundogan	8	2	0	0	10
Rodrigo	7	0	0	0	7
Jack Grealish	3	2	0	1	6
Aymeric Laporte	4	0	0	0	4
Nathan Ake	2	0	0	1	3
Joao Cancelo	1	0	0	2	3
Cole Palmer	0	1	1	1	3
Ferran Torres	2	0	1	0	3
Fernandinho	2	0	0	0	2
Ruben Dias	2	0	0	0	2
John Stones	1	1	0	0	2
Kyle Walker	0	0	0	1	1

Players transferred in for 2021-22

| Jack Grealish | Aston Villa | August 2021 |
| Scott Carson | Derby County | July 2021 |

Trophies won

Premier League

Premier League
Manager of the Month awards

November 2021
December 2021

Stats from the 2021-22 Premier League season:

– *Kevin De Bruyne was our top scorer in the league, with 15 goals, while Riyad Mahrez was our top scorer altogether, with 24 goals in total.*

– *With 2,951, Joao Cancelo made the most passes in the Premier League. Manchester City players also took second and third places in the chart, thanks to Aymeric Laporte (2,920) and Rodri (2,865).*

– *Ederson was the goalkeeper with the joint-highest number of clean sheets, claiming 20 (equal with Ederson) in the league.*

– *Our biggest win was 7-0, which came against Leeds in the Premier League in December.*